Nelson Literacy

Senior Author
Jennette MacKenzie

Consulting Authors
Don Aker
Phil Davison
Michael Kunka
Janeen Werner-King

Publishing Consultant
Joe Banel

Series Consultants
Eldred Barnes, *Instruction*
Damian Cooper, *Assessment*
Sid de Haan, *Technology*
Gayle Gregory, *Differentiated Instruction*
Ruth McQuirter Scott, *Language Conventions*

Series Writing Team

Neil Andersen, *Media Literacy*   Sue Quennell, *Language Conventions*
Maureen Innes, *ELL/ESL*   Janet Lee Stinson, *Instruction*
Kathy Lazarovits, *ELL/ESL*   Michael Stubitsch, *Instruction*

Specialist Reviewer
Brenda Davis, *Education Consultant*
Six Nations of the Grand River

NELSON

NELSON

Nelson Literacy 10a

Vice President, Publishing
Janice Schoening

Executive Publisher,
Literacy and Reference
Michelle Kelly

Managing Editor, Development
Lara Caplan

Senior Program Manager
Diane Robitaille

Program Manager
Anita Reynolds MacArthur

Developmental Editors
Anthony Luengo
Laurie Thomas

Bias Reviewer
Nancy Christoffer

Editorial Assistants
Hannah Gifford
Jennifer Stanicak

Director, Content
and Media Production
Carol Martin

Content Production Editor
Adele Reynolds

Copyeditor
Sandra Manley

Proofreader
Elizabeth d'Anjou

Production Manager
Helen Jager Locsin

Production Coordinator
Vicki Black

Design Director
Ken Phipps

Series Design
Sasha Moroz

Series Wordmark
Sasha Moroz

Cover Design
Jan-John Rivera
Sasha Moroz

Interior Design
Jarrel Breckon
Courtney Hellam
InContext Publishing
Jennifer Laing
Jennifer Leung
Dennis Liwag
Sasha Moroz
Jan-John Rivera
Carianne Sherriff
Craig Wing-King

Art Coordinator
Suzanne Peden

Compositors
Courtney Hellam
Carianne Sherriff

Photo Research and Permissions
Jessie Coffey

Nelson Literacy Series Advisers and Reviewers

Susan Anderson-Coyle, Calgary Board of Education, AB

Charles Baker, Coquitlam SD, BC

Danika Barker, Thames Valley DSB, ON

Mary Bruggeman, Calgary Separate SD, AB

Cheryl Caldwell, Niagara DSB, ON

Myfanwy Charles, Durham DSB, ON

Pamela Collins, Eastern SD, NL

Tina Conlon, Niagara CDSB, ON

Carolyn Craven, Hamilton-Wentworth DSB, ON

Ian Esquivel, Toronto DSB, ON

Jamie Falcone, Halifax Regional SB, NS

Therese Forsythe, Annapolis Valley Regional SB, NS

Wanda Fougere, Mulgrave PD Centre, NS

Nadine Gammon, Calgary Board of Education, AB

Lynda Gellner, Regina Public School Division, SK

Julie Hart, Hamilton-Wentworth DSB, ON

Ben Hazzard, Lambton-Kent SB, ON

Irene Heffel, Edmonton SD, AB

Katherine Kedey, York Region DSB, ON

Shalane Kelsey, Limestone DSB, ON

Linda King, Eastern SD, NL

Jennifer Kozak, Edmonton Public DSB, AB

Raymond Hamilton Lavery, Independent Consultant, MB

Jeanette MacDonald, Calgary RCSSD, AB

Beverley May, District 2, NL

John Merlini, Halton CDSB, ON

Paula Moffat, Eastern Ontario CDSB, ON

Lorellie Munson, York Region DSB, ON

Elen Nika, Delta SD, BC

Vincent O'Brien, Simcoe Muskoka CDSB, ON

Linda O'Reilly, Educational Consultant, BC

Lisa Ottenbreit, North Vancouver SD, BC

Joan Porter, Chignecto-Central Regional SB, NS

Joanne Richardson-Landry, Annapolis Valley Regional SB, NS

Elaine Rose, Ottawa-Carleton DSB, ON

Lindsay Rowley, Delta SD, BC

Carolyn Salonen, Waterloo Region DSB, ON

Sue Schleppe, School District 42, BC

Sharon Seslija, Greater Essex County DSB, ON

Sherry Skinner, Eastern SD, NL

Alison Smith, Delta SD, BC

Diane M. Stevens, Delta SD, BC

Mary Stilwell, School District 6, NB

Janet Lee Stinson, Simcoe County DSB, ON

Melisa Strimas, Bruce-Grey CDSB, ON

Elizabeth Stymiest, District 15, NB

Bob Turner, Greater Saskatchewan CSD, SK

Steven Van Zoost, Annapolis Valley Regional SB, NS

Ann Varty, Trillium Lakelands DSB, ON

Mandy Wamboldt, School District of Mystery Lake, MB

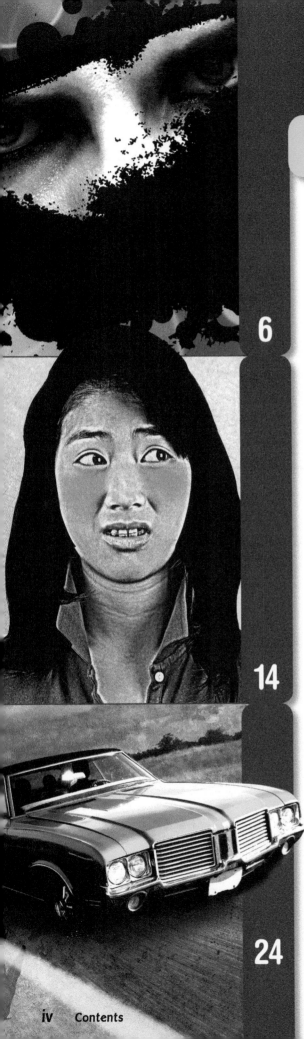

Contents

Unit 1 — Conflict

Contents

Unit 2 — What's the Big Idea?

102

112

124

Welcome to
Nelson Literacy

Nelson Literacy presents a rich variety of literature, informational articles, and media texts from Canada and around the world. Many of the selections offer tips to help you develop strategies in reading, writing, listening, speaking, and media literacy.

Here are the different kinds of pages you will see in this book:

Focus pages

These pages outline a specific strategy and describe how to use it. Included are "Transfer Your Learning" tips that show how you can apply that strategy to other strands and subjects.

Understanding Strategies

These selections have instructions in the margins that help you to understand and use reading, writing, listening, speaking, and media literacy strategies.

Applying Strategies

These selections give you the chance to apply the strategies you have learned. You will see a variety of formats and topics.

Unit Wrap Up

This page provides you with a chance to reflect on your thinking and learning.

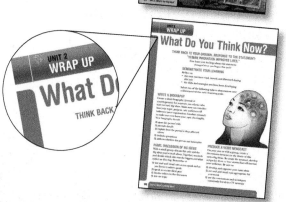

CONFLICT

What do *you* think?

To be human is to experience conflict.				
Strongly Disagree				**Strongly Agree**
1	2	3	4	5

Unit Learning Goals

- making connections
- making inferences
- analyzing elements of short stories
- interpreting media messages
- developing and organizing ideas for writing
- using active listening strategies
- using appropriate vocal strategies

CONFLICT

"You can't shake hands with a clenched fist."
—Indira Gandhi

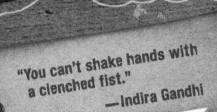

SAY **NO** TO FUR!

SAY **YES** TO FAUX FUR

Anishinabe Elder Walks for Great Lakes

Josephine Mandamin walks 17 000 km in six years to protest environmental collapse

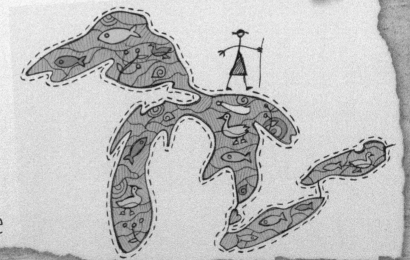

In Flanders Fields

**Poem Excerpt by
Lieutenant Colonel John McCrae**

In Flanders fields the poppies blow
Between the crosses, row on row,
That mark our place; and in the sky
The larks, still bravely singing, fly
Scarce heard amid the guns below.

Canadian Forces Part of UN Peacekeeping Mission

1500 troops heading to conflict zone

How to

MAKE CONNECTIONS

The more you already know about a topic, the better you will understand what you read about it. Making connections with what you are reading is a strategy that helps you activate your prior knowledge (what you already know). Making connections also helps you respond to a text and remember what you have read.

Effective readers make different types of connections.

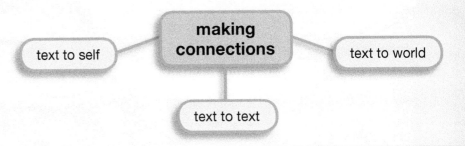

Reading Tip

Connections are not useful if they draw you away from a text and make you forget about what you are reading. As you make connections, ask yourself if they are helping you understand what you are reading. If not, reread that part of the text and try to make a different type of connection.

TYPE OF CONNECTION	HOW TO MAKE THE CONNECTION	EXAMPLES
text to self	Think about the parts of the text that remind you of experiences and people in your own life.	"This character reminds me of my *best* friend, who has the same weird sense of humour. I wonder if this character will also get into trouble because of her sense of humour."
text to text	Think about the parts of the text that remind you of other texts you have read or media you have viewed.	"This magazine article reminds me of a really good documentary I watched about urban violence, so I know the issue has more perspectives than the article suggests."
text to world	Think about the parts of the text that remind you of things you already know (or believe you know) about the world.	"The character in this comedy reminds me of Barack Obama. I wonder if the writer wanted me to make that connection?"

MAKE INFERENCES

When you make inferences, you make assumptions and draw conclusions based on what is actually stated in the text and what you already know. Make inferences while reading to

- draw conclusions about the writer's audience and purpose
- figure out the meaning of a word from how it is used
- figure out relationships between people
- predict and draw conclusions about the people or characters
- figure out who is speaking when a speaker is not identified
- "hear" voice in dialogue or other written statements
- recognize biases of the writer or the characters
- visualize details about an event or setting
- recognize shifts in time and setting
- answer questions raised but not answered by the writer

Reading Tip

Your inferences are based on the connections you make, so everyone makes different inferences. It's easier to make inferences after you make connections. Your initial inferences may or may not be accurate, so be willing to change them as you read.

Connect and Infer

text — connect and infer — prior knowledge

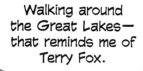

Walking around the Great Lakes—that reminds me of Terry Fox.

Yeah, I figure to do that you'd have to be really dedicated to your cause.

Transfer Your Learning

Connect to ...

History: How has making connections helped you when reading about historic people or events?

Careers: Scientists make inferences and draw conclusions from careful observations. Suggest other careers in which the ability to make inferences is important. In what specific ways is this ability important in those careers?

VOCABULARY

elusive: difficult to define or describe

pelt: the skin of an animal with the fur or hair still on it

PR: a short form for *public relations*, the art or science of establishing a favourable relationship with the public

salvageable: able to be rescued

Vocabulary Tip

PR is an example of an acronym, a word formed from the first letters or syllables of other words. Some acronyms, such as *DVD*, *NATO*, or *TV*, have become so familiar that we seldom use the longer versions.

What do you think?

It's always better to avoid conflict.

Strongly Disagree				Strongly Agree
1	2	3	4	5

The Trickster

Short Story by Jacqueline Pearce

Josh eased into the last empty seat on the bus, trying not to jostle the cardboard box he carried. The top flaps wouldn't close properly, and he was afraid the smell might leak out. He wished he hadn't agreed to go to the university to pick the stuff up for his mom. Lately, he hated going anywhere on the bus or Skytrain—since those guys had jumped him to steal his leather jacket. The last thing he wanted to do was draw attention to himself. What if someone asked him about the box? He imagined the conversation.

"What's in the box?"

"A dead coyote."

"Huh?"

"I'm serious. A deceased …" What had that woman at the university called it? *Canis latrans.* You know, Latin for "barking dog."

Josh thought back to the meeting at the university. His mom had needed the coyote skull and pelt for a project she was doing with her Grade 6 class. She'd persuaded Josh to go for her. Finding the resource centre in the corridors of the science building was like trying to find a tiny piece of cheese in a maze. (Rats, mice, cats, roadrunners … that's what coyotes ate, wasn't it?) The room Josh finally entered was lined floor to ceiling with books. One wall was covered with shelves of stuffed dead animals. A raccoon. An owl. Lots of smaller birds. At the back of the room, a young woman was bent over a desk, writing.

"Excuse me. I'm here to pick up some coyote stuff."

"Oh, hi. Right. Just a minute." She stood up and disappeared into a back room. Whoa, she was good-looking. OK, she was at least five years older than he was, but that could work, couldn't it? Maybe this wouldn't be a wasted afternoon after all. Josh wondered if he could pass for a university student. Try and sound older, smarter. What was some of that stuff mom had been babbling about coyotes? They were related to wolves, foxes, even dogs. They hunted in packs, usually—except for when they lived in the city. Yeah, that's right. City coyotes usually lived alone—or with a mate. He liked the sound of that last word.

"Here you go. One *Canis latrans*," she said, setting down a bundle of yellow-brown fur on the counter, along with a white skull.

"What?" Josh asked, stupidly.

"It's the Latin name," she explained. "It means 'barking dog'."

Something small, grey-white, and pointed rolled across the counter. She picked it up.

"Oh, if any of the teeth fall out, just stick them back in."

She folded the skull and pelt together and wrapped them with tissue paper. Then she bent down behind the counter and came back up with the box.

Josh cleared his throat. OK, maybe he'd had a bad start, but things were still salvageable. *Say something, you idiot.*

"Ah, so do you get a lot of demand for dead coyotes?" Oh, that was brilliant.

She smiled, carefully stuffing the bundle into the box. "Not exactly," she said. "Though a lot of people seem to prefer them dead to alive."

He could tell by the way she said this that she was not one of those people.

"I guess they have a bit of a PR problem," he said, aiming for what he hoped was a kind of intellectual humour.

"You could say that." She seemed to appreciate his comment. "It's true they have lowered the city cat population a bit. But they've lowered the rat population a lot more."

← **Making Connections**

As you read, make connections to help you make inferences. Have you ever been in a situation where you wanted to appear older? Use that connection to help you make inferences about how Josh is feeling.

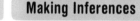

← **Making Inferences**

Make inferences while reading by combining information in the text with what you already know. What do you already know about coyotes that would help you make inferences about why some people would prefer coyotes dead to alive?

"Right," Josh nodded.

"It's ironic," she went on. "Coyotes are one of the few wild animals that have expanded their numbers and territory— despite people trying to get rid of them. It's because they're so good at adapting to things. That's why they can move into the city and do so well."

"Plus, they're not picky eaters," Josh put in. She laughed.

Josh was beginning to feel that maybe things were going all right between them, after all. Adaptable, he thought. That's me. Fitting in with university students wasn't so tough. She handed him the box, still smiling. He pictured the hunting coyote, senses alert, ready to pounce.

"Do you want to go for a coffee?" he asked her straight out.

"I'd love to."

OK, so that last bit was how he rewrote the conversation afterward, sitting on the bus. In actual fact, he'd taken the box from her and sputtered something like, "See you around." As he'd left, he imagined the coyote again. Ahead of the coyote, a rat ran down the alley and scuttled under a fence. Once out of the building, Josh realized he'd been wearing his Fraser High School jacket the whole time. What an idiot.

Josh squirmed mentally in the bus seat. Of course he was wearing the dumb high school jacket instead of his leather one. Even when he managed to put getting mugged the other night out of his mind, it still came back to stalk him.

He'd been on his way to Nick's house around nine o'clock, got off at the Skytrain stop, and there they were. Four guys about his age, leaning against the railing by the steps to the street.

"Hey, nice jacket," one of the guys said. He had a dark, narrow face and wore a blue bandana tied around the top of his head. Two other guys stepped toward him.

"Why don't you give us your jacket?"

Making Inferences

Make inferences about characters by thinking about what they say, think, or do. What can you infer about Josh's character from fantasies such as this one?

Elements of Style

Fiction writers often include flashbacks recounting events that happened earlier. What does this flashback reveal about Josh? What can you infer about Josh's character from this flashback?

At first, Josh thought maybe they were joking. He laughed. OK, well, he tried to laugh. It sounded more like a squeaky door imitation.

"You laughing at us?" All four pressed in on him. There was something tight and coiled up about them. As if they could let go and do anything. Josh glanced around. The Skytrain stop and the surrounding street looked deserted.

The guy with the bandana shoved him. He fell against a big guy who felt kind of soft.

"You looking for a fight?"

"Just a minute." Josh took off his leather jacket—not to give it to them, just to free up his arms. He dropped the coat and sprang into Kung Fu readiness.

OK, so that's where the replay deviated a bit from what actually happened that night. In actual fact, he'd dropped the jacket and run.

On the bus, Josh wondered what the woman at the university would have thought of him if she'd known what happened that night—how shaken up he'd been. He still felt unnerved, off balance. He couldn't even go out of the house without looking over his shoulder. He felt uncomfortable around people in a way he hadn't before. All because of some jerks. His stomach twisted with frustration and anger. Part of him wished he could have fought them and hurt them. He felt like a coward for giving up his jacket so easily and running. But then, on the other hand, running was not so stupid. He was still in one piece, wasn't he? So what if he had lost an expensive piece of clothing? He'd done what he needed to do to survive—like the coyote.

Josh tried to concentrate his thoughts on the woman in the biology museum and forget about the other stuff. It was a much better memory. Maybe she had known he was in high school, but he'd still had a good conversation with a great-looking older woman who hadn't even cared that he was younger. Maybe he could feel good about the whole thing after all.

Making Inferences

Infer the meaning of a word by figuring out how it is used in a passage. What can you infer about the meaning of the word *deviated*?

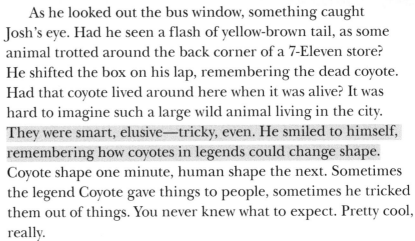

Making Connections

Make text-to-text connections to help you understand the characters and events in a story. This author wants readers to connect to Trickster legends. How is your understanding of the story affected by making that connection (or not making it)?

As he looked out the bus window, something caught Josh's eye. Had he seen a flash of yellow-brown tail, as some animal trotted around the back corner of a 7-Eleven store? He shifted the box on his lap, remembering the dead coyote. Had that coyote lived around here when it was alive? It was hard to imagine such a large wild animal living in the city. They were smart, elusive—tricky, even. He smiled to himself, remembering how coyotes in legends could change shape. Coyote shape one minute, human shape the next. Sometimes the legend Coyote gave things to people, sometimes he tricked them out of things. You never knew what to expect. Pretty cool, really.

Josh looked up. At the front of the bus, a group of girls was getting on. Across the street from the bus, Josh could see a bunch of kids spilling out of a pizza/video-game place. Three guys were leaning against a shiny black Mazda parked in front. Suddenly, with a sick feeling, Josh recognized them. One wore a blue bandana just like the other night. One was wearing a leather jacket just like the one Josh had lost. Josh's first instinct was to duck, melt into the seat. His heart pounded.

Cautiously, he looked again. There was the fourth guy, talking to a girl with long brown hair. She was holding on to his arm as if she wanted to keep him with her, but he was shaking his head and pulling away. The other three guys got into the car. The fourth guy tried to kiss the girl, but she didn't seem to want to kiss him back. He hesitated, then shrugged and turned to join the others. The bus started to move then. Josh could still see the girl standing on the sidewalk, arms crossed, watching the black car pull away. She didn't look happy.

Josh realized he was sweating. He'd been afraid of seeing them again and now he had—he'd seen them, and nothing had happened. It was weird how ordinary they seemed. It almost gave him a feeling of power to know that he'd watched part of their lives—perhaps even knew something about them—and they hadn't even seen him.

A screech of tires drew Josh's attention to the window again. The black car had made a U-turn and was now picking up speed and passing the bus. He wondered where they were going, what they were planning to do.

It was almost dark out now, and the bus's progress was painfully slow. Finally, the bus pulled up next to the Skytrain station where Josh got off. From here, he could transfer to another bus for a five-minute trip home or walk the rest of the way. It was a twenty-minute wait until the next bus. Might as well walk. Josh stepped out of the lighted area onto the dark sidewalk.

It was then that he saw them. They were leaning on the black Mazda, parked where they could watch people come and go from the Skytrain and buses. Josh's heart jumped, and his hands on the box grew immediately sweaty. What were they doing here? Had they followed him? No, they couldn't have. Cruising Skytrain stops was their thing, wasn't it? Seeing them now was just a coincidence, right? They were just here waiting for some poor victim to walk off into the dark alone—like he'd just done. Maybe he could get around the corner before they even noticed. Too late. They were coming.

Josh kept walking, forcing himself to stay calm. Maybe they wouldn't bother him. Maybe they were just going somewhere in this direction. Maybe cows could fly. Who was he kidding?

Images flashed in his mind. The coyote, the rat, himself holding the box, the coyote again—one image transforming into another.

"What's in the box?" The guy with the bandana had come up on one side of Josh. They pressed closer. It was like in the nightmares he'd been having. Someone shoved him.

"We asked you, what's in the box?"

Josh turned to look at the guy who'd spoken. It was the one with the girlfriend. Josh remembered how he'd looked on the street with her—pleading, apologetic. Now, he was changed—swaggering, confident. The others, too, had an edge to them that hadn't been there before. They'd seemed like ordinary individual guys then. Now they were something else—tied together, fuelling each other.

← **Making Inferences**

Make inferences to help you figure out the relationships between people. What can you infer about the relationship between the guys confronting Josh?

Josh felt like a cornered animal. He thought of the fragile skull being pulled out, smashed on the ground. He thought of himself running again—running and running, always looking over his shoulder. Anger flared in his gut, then was gone. He realized he no longer felt afraid. Instead, he felt sort of numb and strangely detached.

Hands grabbed for the box. Josh felt a small click inside himself—like something moved, shifted, and snapped into a new place. With one easy movement, he opened the box flaps and reached his right hand inside. Carefully, he placed his fingers on the furred nose of the pelt head and the skull beneath it. For a moment, the bodies around him drew back, giving space. Swiftly Josh drew out his hand, gripping fur and bone. He thrust the grinning coyote head in one guy's face and growled. It was a deep, menacing animal sound—not human at all.

"I am Coyote," a gravelly voice rose out of the dark, authoritative and mocking. It finished the statement with a sharp yipping howl. What the …? Had he actually just howled?

"I have other names, too," the voice continued. "You don't know me, but I know you. I know everything about you—where you live, what school you go to … Livingston High School," the coyote voice hissed. Josh heard several sharp intakes of breath. Someone laughed, but it sounded nervous. Josh wondered why they didn't do something. The whole thing was crazy. He was crazy.

The pelt moved again, the tips of the hairs shining for a moment in the dark. Josh felt himself take two steps. They were no longer pressing in on him.

"I know a brown-haired girl who wants you to play," the coyote teeth flashed in front of the fourth guy. "You keep leaving her, you're going to lose her.…"

"Hey, how does he …?"

Josh turned again, facing the guy with the leather jacket. The guy glanced toward the car, as if he'd rather be getting in it than standing so close to Josh.

Making Inferences →

Make inferences to figure out which character is speaking when a speaker is not actually identified. Who speaks this line? How do you know that?

"You shouldn't wear things that aren't yours," the coyote voice chided. "Someone might not like it."

"Come on." The guy with the bandana said. His voice sounded deflated. "Let's go … this guy's nuts."

"Yeah, this is getting boring." The guy with the leather jacket turned away, started walking in the direction of the waiting car. Josh could hardly believe they were actually walking away.

The coyote pelt continued to jerk and move, the voice yipping softly, as the four guys climbed into the black car. The engine revved, and the car pulled away from the curb with a squeal.

Josh dropped his arm and let out a long breath. He bent down to set the cardboard box on the sidewalk so he could fold the coyote pelt back inside. His knees felt suddenly weak, and his hands were shaking. He looked at the pale skull in his hands. A moment before it had seemed so full of power— so alive.

Something small and whitish *tinked* onto the sidewalk and rolled in a short arc. A tooth. Josh laughed, feeling close to normal again. He picked up the tooth and placed it back in the coyote's jaw. Ahead of him the street was dark, but he didn't mind. He began walking, feeling a prickle of elation rise up his neck. He tilted his head back and howled—a laughing, yowling, animal-human sound.

Responding

What Do You Think Now? "It's always better to avoid conflict." Has your opinion changed about this statement after reading "The Trickster"? Why or why not? How do you think Josh would respond?

Making Connections: Have you, or anyone you know, ever been bullied or mugged? How does that experience help you respond to Josh's character? What else have you read that connects to the events or characters in this story?

Making Inferences: Make inferences about how the teen with the leather jacket is feeling and what he is thinking when Josh becomes the coyote. What details in the story suggest the teen's thoughts and feelings?

Reading Like a Writer: Reread the last paragraph of the story. Why do you think the author included the details about the tooth at this point?

Media Literacy: If you were casting the role of Josh in a short film based on "The Trickster," what physical and character traits would you look for when choosing the actor? Why?

Evaluating: How effectively do you think the author depicts conflict in this story? Support your answer with evidence from the text.

Metacognition: Which reading strategy—making connections or making inferences—helped you understand the story better as you read? Explain.

VOCABULARY

fungus: mushrooms

prawns: shrimps

Vocabulary Tip
Words that have Latin origins sometimes have unusual plural forms. The plural of "fungus," for example, is "fungi," although more usually, "funguses" is used.

FISH CHEEKS

Personal Anecdote by Amy Tan

I fell in love with the minister's son the winter I turned fourteen. He was not Chinese, but as white as Mary in the manger. For Christmas I prayed for this blond-haired boy, Robert, and a slim new American nose.

When I found out that my parents had invited the minister's family over for Christmas Eve dinner, I cried. What would Robert think of our shabby *Chinese* Christmas? What would he think of our noisy *Chinese* relatives who lacked proper American manners? What terrible disappointment would he feel upon seeing not a roasted turkey and sweet potatoes but *Chinese* food?

On Christmas Eve I saw that my mother had outdone herself in creating a strange menu. She was pulling black veins out of the backs of fleshy prawns. The kitchen was littered with appalling mounds of raw food: A slimy rock cod with bulging fish eyes that pleaded not to be thrown into a pan of hot oil. Tofu, which looked like stacked wedges of rubbery white sponges. A bowl soaking dried fungus back to life. A plate of squid, their backs crisscrossed with knife markings so they resembled bicycle tires.

And then they arrived—the minister's family and all my relatives in a clamour of doorbells and rumpled Christmas packages. Robert grunted hello, and I pretended he was not worthy of existence.

Dinner threw me deeper into despair. My relatives licked the ends of their chopsticks and reached across the table, dipping them into the dozen or so plates of food. Robert and his family waited patiently for platters to be passed to them. My relatives murmured with pleasure when my mother brought out the whole steamed fish. Robert grimaced. Then my father poked his chopsticks just below the fish eye and plucked out the soft meat. "Amy, your favourite," he said, offering me the tender fish cheek. I wanted to disappear.

At the end of the meal my father leaned back and belched loudly, thanking my mother for her fine cooking. "It's a polite Chinese custom to show you are satisfied," explained my father to our astonished guests. Robert was looking down at his plate with a reddened face. The minister managed to muster up a quiet burp. I was stunned into silence for the rest of the night.

After everyone had gone, my mother said to me, "You want to be the same as American girls on the outside." She handed me an early gift. It was a miniskirt in beige tweed. "But inside you must always be Chinese. You must be proud you are different. Your only shame is to have shame."

And even though I didn't agree with her then, I knew that she understood how much I had suffered during the evening's dinner. It wasn't until many years later—long after I had gotten over my crush on Robert—that I was able to fully appreciate her lesson and the true purpose behind one particular menu. For Christmas Eve that year, she had chosen all my favourite foods.

DID YOU KNOW?

American author Amy Tan is a member of the rock band Rock Bottom Remainders. Members include mystery writer Barbara Kingsolver, *The Simpsons* creator Matt Groening, humour columnist Dave Barry, and writer Stephen King.

eBook*Extra*

Responding

What Do You Think Now? After reading Amy Tan's personal anecdote, do you think fitting in is more important than being yourself? Explain.

Making Connections: Which kinds of connections did you find yourself making the most: text-to-self, text-to-text, or text-to-world? Explain with specific references to the text.

Making Inferences: What can you infer from the use of the word *then* in the line, "And even though I didn't agree with her then ..."?

Reading Like a Writer: Reread the paragraph about food preparation beginning with, "On Christmas Eve, I saw that my mother had outdone herself...." Identify the specific details that help bring that scene to life.

Critical Literacy: This event occurred in the mid 1960s. How does the context for this selection affect its content? How might the selection change if it were to happen today in a Canadian home?

Metacognition: What made this anecdote easy or difficult to understand? What strategies helped you understand it?

VOCABULARY

Ba'ath Party: the ruling political party in Iraq under Saddam Hussein; the party was named after the Arabic word for "resurrection"

Vocabulary Tip

Remember that many words have multiple meanings. If one meaning doesn't work in a specific context, think of others. For example, the word *party* also means an organized group of people, as in a political party.

What do you think?

Should citizens who face conflict within their own countries be allowed to enter other countries? Explain.

B., 16

Memoir recorded by Deborah Ellis

B. is an anonymous 16-year-old boy interviewed by Deborah Ellis for her book *Children of War: Voices of Iraqi Refugees.*

B. was born in Iraq, where his father had a successful business. That business was confiscated by the Iraqi government and his father's life was in danger. B. and his family fled to Jordan.

Ankara
TURKEY

CYPRUS Nicosia

Tehran

Mediterranean Sea

LEBANON **SYRIA**
Beirut Damascus Baghdad

IRAN

ISRAEL
Jerusalem Amman **IRAQ**

JORDAN

Cairo
KUWAIT Kuwait

Persian Gulf

EGYPT

SAUDI ARABIA Doha Abu Dhabi

QATAR
Riyadh
UNITED ARAB EMIRATES

Red Sea

OMAN

My brother was caught working here in Jordan, and he was sent back to Iraq. That's why you can't take my picture or use my real name. That's why I never leave the house. I feel that the immigration police are out there watching for me and waiting for me to make a mistake. Then they will grab me. People tell me I am wrong about this, that there are so many Iraqis here the police don't have time to worry about me, that there are lots of others they can catch. To them I say, so where is my brother? And to that they have no answer.

I am almost a man, but I have no work, I have no future. My hair is already turning grey. When I was young, I wanted to be a famous football player. I feel foolish now for having that dream.

I have been in Jordan with my family for nine years. We live in Zarqa, a crowded, noisy place outside Amman. Our house is a poor house without even a proper ceiling. It's all reeds and we've put plastic under the reeds to keep out the rain and the dust, but it doesn't work that well.

My life was not supposed to be like this. I was supposed to have a different future. My father is a goldsmith. He learned the trade from his father, who learned it from his father, who learned it from his father, back many, many generations. I was supposed to be learning the trade in my father's goldsmith shop in Baghdad, but the shop doesn't exist anymore.

When my father was younger he was a very important goldsmith. He went on trips to Bulgaria and other European places, showing people what he could do. The shop was very successful, and we were very rich. We had a beautiful house, many possessions, cars, everything anyone would want. Now look at us! Even the rugs on the floor came from someone else's garbage out in the street.

My father's shop was taken by Saddam because my father refused to join the Ba'ath Party. Saddam considered him a traitor, took away his shop and threatened to hang him. So we left. We have been in Jordan since before the Americans came. I had to leave school in the sixth grade, and have not been back.

Now my father is very sick. He has diabetes, very bad, and he had to have his leg cut off. They gave him an artificial leg, but he lost a lot of weight, so the leg no longer fits. He usually manages without it, hobbling around on his crutches.

His heart is bad, too. His heart problems became worse when my brother was arrested.

My brother was selling cigarettes in the streets and markets around Zarqa. It wasn't much of a job, but it brought in a little money to help feed us. The Jordanian immigration police grabbed him and said, "Show us your papers!" He didn't have any papers because we're not legal to be in Jordan.

The police brought him back to us in handcuffs and told him to quickly pack a few things. Then they drove him to the Iraq border. We heard from him later that he was met there by American soldiers. He said they treated him well. They let him wash, gave him a bit of money and food. Now he's staying with relatives in Al Kut, two hours from Baghdad. He doesn't do anything there. Just misses us.

My sister lives with us, too. She is older than me and married, although her husband has disappeared. We don't know if he is dead or in prison or what. Maybe the police got him and deported him, or maybe he was just tired of taking care of so many people and went away. We don't know. My sister and her baby live here with us.

We keep to ourselves. We don't want to draw attention.

I don't know where my life will go. Should I go back to Iraq and be with my brother? I hardly know Iraq, and I would have no job there. My only hope is if I can get out of Jordan and start life fresh in a new country, somewhere far away, somewhere new.

I really try not to think. When I think, I am too much reminded of what I've lost, and then it's like I fall into a deep, deep pit, with no way out.

eBook Extra

Responding

What Do You Think Now? "Should citizens who face conflict within their own countries be allowed to enter other countries?" How do you respond now that you've read the selection? How do you think a citizen of Jordan would respond after talking with B.?

Making Connections: Have you read other texts or viewed a media text in which a person felt trapped? If yes, how did this influence your understanding as you read this selection? If no, were you able to imagine yourself being confined for years? Explain.

Making Inferences: B. probably responded to questions asked by Deborah Ellis. Choose a passage and suggest a question that he was responding to.

Critical Literacy: Reread the selection again, this time without the introduction. Do you think the introduction is necessary? Why or why not?

Metacognition: Did you find yourself looking at the images in this selection before, during, or after reading? How did the images support your understanding of the selection?

What do you think?

In a conflict between humans and nature, which side is likely to win?

Canadian January Night

Poem by Alden Nowlan

VOCABULARY

phosphorescent: glowing

Vocabulary Tip

Visualize the scene to help you understand new words: "cars/slide like phosphorescent beetles."

Ice storm; the hill
pyramid of black crystal
down which the cars
slide like phosphorescent beetles
while I, walking backwards in obedience
to the wind, am possessed
of the fearful knowledge
my compatriots share
but almost never utter:
this is a country
where a man can die
simply from being
caught outside.

eBook*Extra*

Responding

What Do You Think Now? "In a conflict between humans and nature, which side is likely to win?" Did reading this poem change your response to this question? Explain.

Making Connections: What experiences have you had that support your reading of this poem?

Making Inferences: What inferences can you make about how the poet feels about being Canadian?

Critical Literacy: How might female readers respond to this poem? Why do you think the poet uses the word *man*?

Literary Devices: Identify the metaphor or the simile in this poem. Explain why it is effective.

Metacognition: How did making inferences help you understand this poem?

How to

ANALYZE THE ELEMENTS OF SHORT STORIES

By cleverly using and combining story elements, writers can create memorable short stories.

PLOT

The plot of a short story is the way in which events in the story are arranged. Usually the plot builds from an introduction of the characters, setting, and problem up through the rising action. Suspense in the story builds as the problem is revealed. The rising action is more like a series of steps than a straight line soaring upward, since tension in the story is often relieved by description or humour. Finally, the story's highest point is reached, the climax, where the characters succeed or fail. Following the climax is the falling action and the resolution, the section of the story in which questions or issues are settled. Sometimes, however, the writer may decide not to resolve things, leaving readers to think of their own possible resolutions.

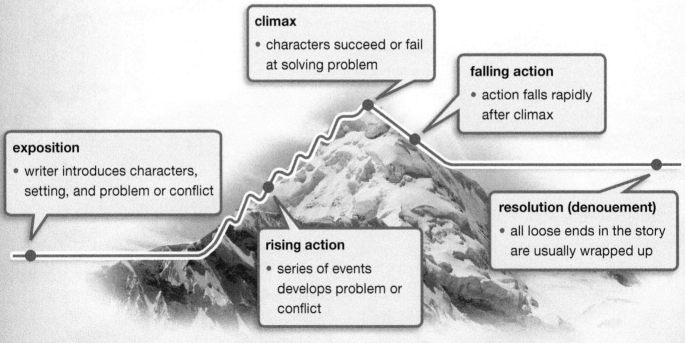

climax
• characters succeed or fail at solving problem

falling action
• action falls rapidly after climax

exposition
• writer introduces characters, setting, and problem or conflict

rising action
• series of events develops problem or conflict

resolution (denouement)
• all loose ends in the story are usually wrapped up

Plot is how authors arrange events in a story. Many stories use the above plot structure. Sometimes stories have an *anticlimax* (an abrupt lapse of tension).

PROBLEM OR CONFLICT

Conflict is a problem or struggle in a story. The main character may come into conflict with a variety of forces, but all can be grouped into one of two types:

- External conflict involves a character struggling against others, society, or nature.
- Internal conflict involves a character having opposing feelings or thoughts about something regarding him or herself.

CHARACTERS

At the centre of every short story is a character who wants something. To catch and keep your attention as a reader, the writer must create a believable conflict that prevents the character from getting this wish (at least for part of the story). The main character of a story is called the protagonist. Whomever or whatever the main character comes into conflict with is called the antagonist.

To create effective short stories, writers must convey a strong sense of their fictional characters.

Writers often play with the **connections** that readers form with a character, making their readers **infer** something about a character that may or may not be true. Reading a short story includes affirming or revising your impression of the main character.

TECHNIQUE FOR DEVELOPING CHARACTER	HOW THIS TECHNIQUE WORKS
thoughts and feelings	A character's thoughts, memories, and reactions reveal what motivates the character.
actions	How a character behaves (for example, kicking someone) reveals the character's values.
dialogue	What a character says and how the character says it reveal his or her personality and relationships.
other characters' comments	We can learn much about a character from what other characters say about him or her.
setting	Imagining a character in a particular setting (for example, an expensive clothing store) immediately shapes a reader's impression.
physical appearance	A scar, a missing tooth, or even the type of clothing a character chooses to wear can create an immediate impression. As the plot develops, however, this impression may turn out to be misleading.

THEME

The theme is the central idea or message of a story. The theme of a story may be stated directly or indirectly. Common story themes include love, fate, courage, death, war, revenge, betrayal. How would you describe the theme of "The Trickster"?

An important point to note about theme is that it can be open to interpretation. Different people will see the same story from different perspectives and so have slightly different interpretations of the theme. One way to interpret a story's theme is to focus on what changes in the story.

WHAT MIGHT CHANGE	WHAT TO LOOK FOR
the main character's situation	The main character might be in a better (or worse) situation at the end of the story than at the beginning.
the main character's thinking and/or behaviour	The main character might change his or her opinion or behaviour about something.
the way you feel about the main character	You might come to respect the main character more (or less) at the end of the story than at the beginning.

STORY ELEMENTS WORK TOGETHER

The relationship between story elements can be more complicated than indicated below, but here's one way of looking at those relationships.

plot ——**drives**——▶ character ——**drives**——▶ plot

setting ——**drives**——▶ character

conflict ——**drives**——▶ plot and character ——**drives**——▶ conflict

theme ——**drives**——▶ plot and conflict

LITERARY DEVICES

Writers of fiction use a variety of literary devices to develop their conflicts and support their readers' understanding of themes.

Symbolism is the use of something to represent more than itself. Fiction writers sometimes use images when they want to convey important ideas. A red rose, for example, could be used to symbolize beauty or love; but a red rose with wilted petals might symbolize faded beauty or lost love.

An analogy is a comparison made between something that is known and something less familiar. The purpose of creating an analogy is to help others better understand a difficult concept or process.

Foreshadowing is a reference that hints about an event that will happen later on in the story. A writer might foreshadow an event directly or indirectly. Foreshadowing can make something seem important, provide information, create suspense, or make an event more believable.

A flashback is an interruption in a work of fiction or drama that presents an earlier event. A flashback is useful when

- writers start their story in the middle to grab the reader's attention. The flashback explains how the event came about.

- it gives readers a better understanding of the characters.

Writers can prepare readers to recognize flashbacks by using phrases such as, "Earlier that day …," or by setting it apart from the rest of the story. Sometimes, though, flashbacks can be harder to recognize. If you find yourself suddenly lost as you are reading a story, ask yourself if the writer has taken you back in time.

foreshadowing

flashback

symbolism

It was a dark and silent night, a night when something *must* happen. It was past midnight, but I was restless, sleepless, anxious, and as jittery as a kid on a chocolate high. I sat down in the kitchen to eat some apple pie and think about how well my life had been going lately. I was trying to calm myself down. It wasn't working.

Suddenly, the doorbell rang, reminding me of the time—three years past—when Target was hit by a car because I'd forgotten to let him back in the house. I never had been able to get the blood stain out of the hall carpet. It was still there—a reproachful blotch—as I approached the front door.

Transfer Your Learning

Connect to …

Oral Communication: How could you use symbolism to help you deliver an oral presentation?

History: What techniques for developing character could a history writer use to bring historical figures to life?

VOCABULARY

cat's paw: a type of crowbar used to pull apart materials

derelicts: wrecks

double-bitted: having two cutting edges

ineptness: incompetence

pinch bar: a type of crowbar

Vocabulary Tip

Understanding the situation can help you understand a new word. You can figure out the word *derelicts* by thinking about the type of vehicles the father takes apart.

What do you think?

How you handle conflict with others defines your relationship with them.

Strongly Disagree				Strongly Agree
1	2	3	4	5

SCARS

Short Story by Don Aker

Understanding Short Stories →

Writers use foreshadowing to hint at events that will happen later in the story. In the first paragraph, how was foreshadowing used?

Understanding Short Stories ↘

A character's actions reveal much about his or her personality. What can you infer about the father's personality from his actions?

The axe was double-bitted. Maybe that was a warning—*double-bitted*: biting twice. First the metal of the old Volkswagen van and then the flesh and bone between my eyes.

My father bought old vehicles and bullied them back to life, transplanting parts from one to the other, then chopping up the derelicts with his axe and hauling them to the dump on the back of his old Fargo. I had none of his mechanical skill. Sometimes I got tools for him, always having to ask if the Robertson screwdriver was the one with the square or the cross. Sometimes I held trouble lights or steadied the block and tackle. Sometimes I turned the ignition while he coaxed, manipulated, or threatened tired parts back into operation. I often wondered why he asked me to help. Even loading the large metal pieces on the back of the truck was something I couldn't do alone, although my father could lift them with ease.

On this particular day, he was dismantling an ancient VW Kombi van in the field behind our house. The August air lay on us like a quilt, and I watched my father's green work shirt grow black with sweat as the axe pistoned up and down. I longed to slip away to the river for a swim, but I knew my father. We would stop when the job was finished.

I looked at the growing pile of scrap metal and felt resentment work its way up my neck in hot waves. I hated being there. Not just because it was a Saturday and it was August, but because the work was a constant reminder of my brother's absence.

My brother, who could make kites out of bread bags, who could build a raft out of poplar saplings and twine, who could fix the radio my father had given him, and who could die in four months from a disease I still couldn't spell.

I hated being there.

"Daniel!"

I turned to see my father staring at me. "What?"

"I need the pinch bar."

I reached toward the tools spread on the grass.

"Not the cat's paw. The pinch bar!"

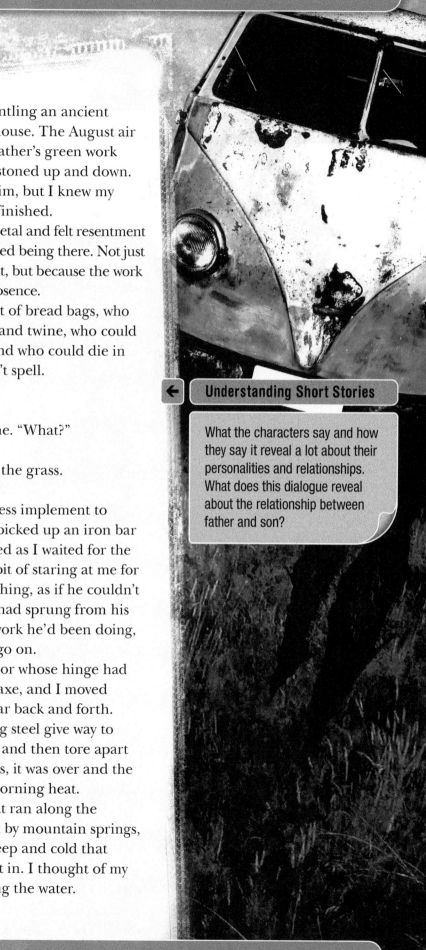

← **Understanding Short Stories**

What the characters say and how they say it reveal a lot about their personalities and relationships. What does this dialogue reveal about the relationship between father and son?

My hands darted from one meaningless implement to another until my father strode over and picked up an iron bar inches from my fingertips. My ears burned as I waited for the look and the silence. My father had a habit of staring at me for a moment when he was angry, saying nothing, as if he couldn't quite believe that I and all my ineptness had sprung from his loins. Then he'd turn away, back to the work he'd been doing, that he was always doing. And we would go on.

He used the pinch bar to pry off a door whose hinge had stubbornly resisted the pounding of the axe, and I moved closer to watch as he worked the metal bar back and forth. This was the only part I enjoyed, watching steel give way to steel, bending and groaning as it rippled and then tore apart in ragged smiles. And then, like all things, it was over and the axe again rose and clanged in the mid-morning heat.

My thoughts returned to the river that ran along the western edge of my father's property. Fed by mountain springs, even the slower water of August was so deep and cold that the only way to bear it was to dive straight in. I thought of my brother, his slim body a white blade slicing the water.

Then the axe struck me.

Understanding Short Stories

The plot of a short story usually has one problem that has to be solved. Finding the solution to that problem occurs during the rising action of the plot. What is the problem in this story? How do you think that problem will be resolved?

I would learn later that the force of the final upward swing pulled the axe from my father's tired, greasy hands; that the metal-reinforced frame of the thick glasses I wore and hated saved my sight and quite possibly my life. But I knew none of this now. I was somehow in that river, floating beneath a crimson sky. Oddly, there was no pain, only a strident jangling inside my head, and I felt myself beginning to sink before I was jerked into awareness by my father.

Shouting my mother's name, he ran to the house with me in his arms. Moments later, all three of us were in our old Cutlass, my mother holding a dishtowel over my face. My father said nothing as he drove, of course. What needed to be said? I'd been standing too close. It was my fault.

When the car skidded to a stop in front of the hospital, I thought about my glasses lying somewhere in the field behind our house. Broken again, no doubt. My father had already paid for a new pair this year. I told him I'd smashed them in gym class and he hadn't discovered my lie, that I'd broken them myself, enjoying the sound the plastic frames made as I twisted them between my hands.

My mother opened her door even before the car stopped moving and, keeping the towel pressed against my forehead, she got out, guiding me behind her.

"I'll park the car," said my father.

My mother hesitated for only a moment. Then, her arm around me, she turned and steered me up the steps and through the large doors. Behind me, I could hear my father's Cutlass driving away.

Emergencies in the county hospital were handled at the outpatients' department. My mother spoke to the woman at the admitting desk. Standing beside her now, I remembered the last time I was there. My brother had been sick for days, and at first we thought it was the flu. My mother could do nothing but wipe his face with a cold cloth as he knelt over the toilet retching and heaving. I remembered lying in bed listening to the strangled coughing followed by the inevitable splash, my own stomach churning. Incredibly, my father slept—until my mother woke him to tell him about the blood. Then we brought him here.

I heard footsteps approach. "Well, that's quite a mess you've got there," came a young woman's voice. Crusted with dried blood, the dishtowel clung to my forehead until she gently eased it away. Everything was a blur and again I thought of my glasses lying in the field behind our house. "How did this happen?" the nurse asked.

"An axe," said my mother. "It was an accident."

"I'll make sure the doctor sees you next. Have a seat in the waiting room."

Three other people were already there, but my near-sighted eyes could make out only their forms. No one spoke as my mother and I sat. Voices echoed everywhere, crying and conversation knitted together by nurses bustling importantly back and forth. A speaker hummed and quietly asked for a maintenance worker to report to the mechanical room, and I thought of my father, who still had not appeared.

← **Understanding Short Stories**

Writers use flashbacks to present earlier events. How is this flashback introduced? Why do you think a flashback is used here?

↙ **Understanding Short Stories**

Seeing a character in a particular setting can shape a reader's impression of that character. How is setting used here to heighten your impression of the main character and his mother?

"How does it feel?" my mother asked.

"Doesn't hurt. How's it look?"

My mother brushed my hair off my forehead. "Swollen quite a bit." Taking something from her purse, she got up and walked down the hall and, in a moment, I could hear the *shir* of a water fountain. She returned carrying a wet handkerchief, which she rubbed gently over my face.

The wetness brought things into clearer focus. My mother's face suddenly looked old, lines like the branches of bare trees on her forehead and under her eyes. But it was the fear in them that surprised me. I had seen that fear the night we brought my brother here. That was the first time I'd realized my mother could be afraid.

The nurse returned. "The doctor can see you," she said.

I saw my mother glance toward the entrance. "You can wait here," I told her.

"No." Her voice was firm. "I'll come with you."

The examining room was blue with two high beds separated by a drawn curtain. From the second came voices, the doctor with another patient speaking in low tones, but I had no desire to listen. My legs were trembling and my face was beginning to wake up, nerve endings whispering about the pain I would feel. My mother stood at the door.

The night we brought my brother here, the on-call doctor immediately admitted him for tests, so my father went to fill out the necessary papers while my mother and I followed a nurse who pushed my brother in a wheelchair to the men's ward. At first I thought it would be better than the children's ward, but most of the patients were old. Someone's grandfather lay in the bed nearest my brother. He was perfectly still from the waist up, his wrists strapped to the bed's metal side-rails, but his legs were in constant motion, hilling and troughing the blankets. I couldn't stop staring at that old man, forever walking with his mouth open and eyes closed, and it was then that I knew my brother was going to die.

Four months later he did.

Understanding Short Stories →

Writers may include a single flashback that recounts an earlier time or they may include several flashbacks throughout the story to differentiate moments of that earlier time. Suggest a reason why the main character's memories are told in several flashbacks rather than in a single flashback.

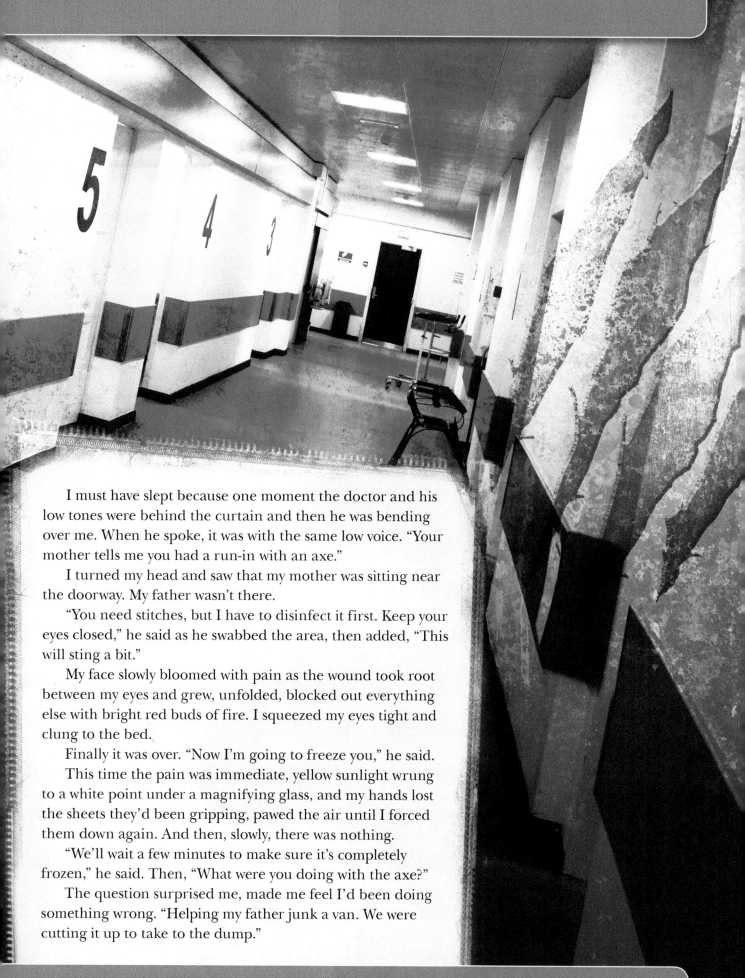

I must have slept because one moment the doctor and his low tones were behind the curtain and then he was bending over me. When he spoke, it was with the same low voice. "Your mother tells me you had a run-in with an axe."

I turned my head and saw that my mother was sitting near the doorway. My father wasn't there.

"You need stitches, but I have to disinfect it first. Keep your eyes closed," he said as he swabbed the area, then added, "This will sting a bit."

My face slowly bloomed with pain as the wound took root between my eyes and grew, unfolded, blocked out everything else with bright red buds of fire. I squeezed my eyes tight and clung to the bed.

Finally it was over. "Now I'm going to freeze you," he said.

This time the pain was immediate, yellow sunlight wrung to a white point under a magnifying glass, and my hands lost the sheets they'd been gripping, pawed the air until I forced them down again. And then, slowly, there was nothing.

"We'll wait a few minutes to make sure it's completely frozen," he said. Then, "What were you doing with the axe?"

The question surprised me, made me feel I'd been doing something wrong. "Helping my father junk a van. We were cutting it up to take to the dump."

He raised his eyebrows. "You must be pretty strong."

"My father is."

"Where's your father now?"

I had no answer to this question. It made me think of Jimmie MacBurnie and his red yarn. Jimmie was the only mentally challenged person I'd ever seen. Thirty-something, he lived with his parents near Taylor Lake where my brother and I used to fish. Often we found pieces of bright red yarn tied to trees a few feet apart around the lake, and we asked my mother about them. "Jimmie puts them there so he can find his way in the woods," she'd said, then warned us not to touch them. A few years earlier, some kids had hidden several pieces as a prank and Jimmie had gotten lost. It had taken a search team all night and the following morning to find him curled up on the ground crying. I thought of Jimmie wandering about looking for that red yarn, knowing it had to be there but not being able to find it—like the answer to the question the doctor was asking me now.

My mother spoke for me. "He went to park the car."

Yes. Except that by now he probably had the hood up and was cleaning the spark plugs or tightening the fan belt. Important things that needed doing. I thought about how my father hadn't come up from the admitting office the night we brought my brother here, although my mother and I stayed in the men's ward over an hour.

I thought about when we'd gotten home from my brother's funeral, listening to my mother crying in the next room while my father went outside to change the oil.

I thought about my mother sitting near the doorway of the examining room now, watching the corridor when she wasn't watching me.

And before I could stop myself, I was crying. Long, uncontrolled sobs that seemed to come from somewhere else, some*one* else. Ashamed, I tried to bury them in the pillow but, muffled, they resembled the sounds my mother still made at night sometimes when she thought everyone was asleep. I cried even harder.

Then my mother was bending over me, her hands stroking my hair.

"It's shock," I heard the doctor say.

My mother said nothing, just kept stroking my hair. I cried for what seemed a long time. And then I couldn't cry anymore.

Understanding Short Stories →

Writers often use analogies to help readers better understand their characters. What's the analogy in this passage? How does it help you understand the narrator's reaction to the doctor's question?

Understanding Short Stories →

A character's thoughts help convey vivid impressions of that character. What do you infer about the main character from this series of thoughts?

"The freezing should be ready now," the doctor said finally. "He won't feel anything." I thought he was probably right.

The stitching didn't take long. This time I kept my eyes open, watching the doctor's smooth hands move deftly over my face. They were nothing like my father's hands, thick and scarred, the nails always dark with grease or oil. These hands were soft and white against the room's blue walls, snowbirds in an October sky. They were like my hands, yet capable and sure. I wondered what my father would think of these hands.

"The stitches should come out in a week," the doctor said to my mother, perhaps afraid I'd burst into tears again. I didn't care. I just wanted it to be over.

And then it was. Ten minutes later, we were outside shielding our eyes against the sudden sun, scanning the parking lot for the car.

"There it is." My mother pointed.

Without my glasses, I knew which car was ours—the hood was up. As we made our way down the steps and over the loose gravel, I stumbled and silently cursed the stones under my feet. Then I cursed the car. And then my father.

← **Understanding Short Stories**

Physical details often convey vivid impressions of a character. How do the descriptions of the characters' hands help convey strong impressions of these characters?

Understanding Short Stories

There are two types of conflict in stories: internal and external. What type of conflict does this story focus on most?

As we approached the Cutlass, I could see his blurred form leaning in under the hood and I wondered what he could possibly have found to fix this time. As we came closer, though, I didn't hear the familiar tap and creak of tools in the act of resurrection and repair. Instead came the crack and snap of something breaking.

I had never seen my father break anything, my father who only ever put together or took apart. Even the dismantling of the vehicles in the field behind our house was purposeful and controlled. The sounds I heard as we walked toward the car were anything but that. I'd heard these sounds before, but their meaning was unclear, blurred like my vision.

His back to us, my father was staring at something in his hands, but he straightened when he heard us coming. Stepping back, he pushed the hood shut, the sound heavy and final. Without turning, he shoved something in his pocket, but the flash of sun off its polished surface told me what he'd been holding, what he'd been breaking.

I was sitting in English class, everyone reciting the parts of speech ("A noun is the name of a person, place, or thing") when the principal had come across the PA telling Mrs. Wheaton that my mother was in the office.

"You may go, Daniel," the teacher said.

But I didn't want to go, didn't want to hear what my mother had to tell me. Instead, I sat there looking at the board, wanting only to crawl inside the safety of those rules that made people and things the same.

"I said you may *go*," she repeated, and there was nothing else I could do.

But I didn't go to the office. I ran for the exit, flying out the door and toward the woods behind the school. Branches lashed my face and arms as I crashed through the trees but I kept running, ploughing through jack pine and cat spruce until I fell headlong into spongy, dark soil.

When I got up, I wasn't wearing my glasses. I had to scratch and paw through leaves and pine needles to find them, unaware I was crying. When my hands finally closed on them, I didn't put them on my face. Instead, I bent back one of the bows like a wishbone and listened to it *crack*, the brown plastic snapping cleanly in two.

My brother had stopped dying.

My brother was dead.

I bent the other bow—this time more slowly—and watched the plastic cloud before it broke. This time the *crack* and *snap* were almost simultaneous. It somehow seemed important that I could do this, that I could make this happen. It made it easier to be angry and afraid and alone.

These were the sounds my father had made under the hood of the Cutlass, made with the glasses he'd gone back and found but would never give me.

I'd expected to go on feeling hurt, expected to feel the fury swell in me like our river during spring melt, but my anger evaporated. I climbed into the back seat while my mother slipped into the front beside my father. He started the car and backed it out of the shade into bright sunlight and we headed home.

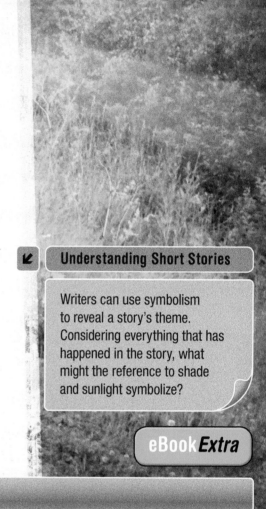

Understanding Short Stories

Writers can use symbolism to reveal a story's theme. Considering everything that has happened in the story, what might the reference to shade and sunlight symbolize?

eBook Extra

Responding

What Do You Think Now? "How you handle conflict with others defines your relationship with them." Think about your own experiences and the story you've just read. Has your answer changed? Explain.

Understanding Short Stories: At the heart of every story is a character who wants something. What does Daniel want? Identify details that support your answer.

Drawing Conclusions: One way to interpret theme is to focus on what changes during the story. What changed in "Scars"? Use your answer to this question and your answer to what shade and sunlight symbolize to figure out the theme of this story.

Literary Devices: Don Aker has used symbolism, foreshadowing, and flashbacks. Choose one of these devices. Identify where it's used and discuss how it supports your understanding of the story.

Critical Thinking: The only physical injury mentioned in the story is the one Daniel receives when he is struck by the axe. Why do you think the author called the story "Scars" instead of "The Scar"?

Metacognition: As you read "Scars," was there any part where you found it difficult to follow what was happening? What did you do to improve your understanding?

VOCABULARY

caterwauling: shrill noise

Peaceable Kingdom: from the Bible, an ideal world in which all living beings live together in harmony

portabella: a variety of mushroom

Vocabulary Tip

Access your prior knowledge to help you figure out new words. For example, if you know something about the behaviour of raccoons at night, you can figure out that caterwauling means making a shrill noise.

Flash fiction is a type of short story that is very brief (300 to 1000 words). These stories may not include all the elements of a short short or may compress the elements into a few lines. This type of story may also be called *short short stories*, *micro-fiction*, *sudden fiction*, or *postcard fiction*.

What do you think?

Conflict can make you compromise your beliefs.

Strongly Disagree				Strongly Agree
1	2	3	4	5

INVASION OF THE SNOTTY

Flash Fiction by Karin Weber

At first she thought they were raccoons: the spilled garbage and nightly caterwauling under the hedge. The next morning clumps of grey fur were lodged in the armpits of her garden angel. Raccoons for sure.

Luckily they ignored her garbage, and went can tipping next door. Pizza rinds and baloney wrap festooned the shared chainlink fence like punk Christmas lights. The neighbours cleaned up their side. They copied her garbage security system of bungee cords, yet night after night their garbage was chosen.

Actually it was irritating. Her can, with its smears of organic humus and tofu, just didn't rate for raiding. She glared out the window at midnight. To her surprise the raccoons were flat and had stumpy tails. Badgers! In suburban Canada? How exciting!

She googled "badgers." They couldn't yawn but they liked corn and mushrooms. She made a portabella stew and promptly threw it out. The next morning an empty bacon package was left under her car. She felt angry.

BADGERS

She adored Nature, religiously recycled, shopped organically, left miniscule footprints wherever she trod, and the Peaceable Kingdom up and supped on crappy food next door.

She put out fresh corn only to be greeted by shredded Pop-Tart boxes on her patio. She raged. Time to shop for new tactics: Froot Loops and Cheez Whiz. While mixing them in a big bowl, she casually licked a finger. Then, as if she had become someone else, she took another intoxicating taste.

eBook Extra

Responding

What Do You Think Now? "Conflict can make you compromise your beliefs." Now that you've read this selection, have you changed your mind? Why or why not?

Understanding Short Stories: Which short story elements did you find worked most effectively in this selection? Support your answer.

Reading for Detail: How would you describe the narrator's diet? Explain why her diet is an important aspect of the selection.

Literary Devices: The title of this selection plays on the title of the classic science fiction movie *Invasion of the Body Snatchers*, in which aliens take over human bodies. How does this pun affect your understanding of the story?

Critical Thinking: How does the author introduce, develop, and resolve the selection in so few words?

Evaluating: What did you like most and what did you like least about this story? Explain.

Metacognition: Did the shortness of the story have an impact on your ability to make connections or inferences? Explain.

VOCABULARY

Fortune 500: the 500 most profitable business corporations in the United States

Vocabulary Tip

Using context can help you understand unfamiliar terms, such as *Fortune 500*. If you think about how CEO means "Chief Executive Officer," and fortune means "wealth," you can work out that Fortune 500 companies are probably very successful, wealthy businesses.

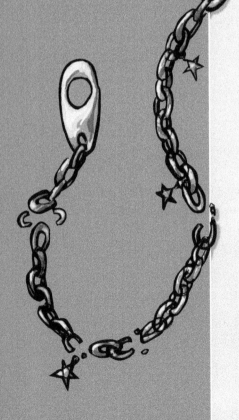

Short Story by Susan Beth Pfeffer

That winter, it felt like every time I saw my father, the sun cast off just a little more warmth than it had the day before. I'd been seeing him Tuesdays for almost two years at that point. Mom, who was still working on completing her degree, took Tuesday and Thursday evening classes, so I'd go straight to Dad's from school, wait for him to show, and then we'd have supper together and talk.

Dad drove me home Tuesday nights, and the moon always shone as brightly as the sun had and the winter stars looked joyful and beckoning. When I was little, Dad used to promise me the stars for a necklace, but like most of his promises, that one never quite happened.

"I'm a dreamer," he said to me more than once, which really wasn't all that different from what Mom said. "He's an irresponsible bum" was her way of wording it. I knew he was both, but I also knew that winter that the sun and the moon dreamed with him.

Sometimes when I haven't seen Dad for a few days, on a Saturday or a Sunday, I'll try to figure out why Mom ever married him. She's the most practical person I know, always putting aside for a rainy day. With Mom, there are a lot of rainy days and she takes a grim sort of pleasure in being ready for them. The flashlight with working batteries for a blackout. The extra quarters when the laundry isn't quite dry. Dad gets by on a grin and a willingness to help. He's always there if you need him. Well, not always.

He's unexpectedly there, like a warm day in January. He's a rescuer. "I saw a woman stranded on the road," he'd say. "So I changed her tire for her." Or he found a wallet with the ID intact, and returned it in person to its owner (and, of course, turned down a reward).

He told me once, "If I've done one thing, no matter how small, that made the world a better place, I'm satisfied. All I can give you is dreams, Ashes. But one good dream is worth a thousand flashlight batteries."

Ashes. I can still hear the fight. It was just a couple of months before the breakup. I was in bed when they went at it.

"Her name is Ashleigh!" Mom shouted. "A name you insisted on. So why do you call her 'Ashes'?"

"That's just my nickname for her," Dad replied. He was always harder to hear when they fought.

"But ashes are cold, grey, dead things," Mom yelled.

"It's just a nickname," Dad repeated, a little quieter.

"You call her that just to annoy me!" Mom yelled, but Dad's reply was so soft, I could no longer hear him.

A couple of days later, when Dad forgot to pick me up at school, or didn't have the money for the class trip, or got all his favourite kinds of Chinese and none of Mom's and mine, I thought maybe Mom was right, and Dad did call me Ashes just to annoy her. I made a list that evening of all the words that rhymed with *ashes*—*smashes* and *crashes*, *trashes* and *bashes*, *clashes* and *mashes*—and it didn't seem quite so nice anymore, having a special nickname. But then Dad gave me roses or sang a song he'd written for me. Or maybe he moved two buses away. And I realized he still called me Ashes, where Mom couldn't hear him to be annoyed. And that made me feel special all over again. Mom might never be caught without batteries or tissues, but she just called me Ashleigh—a name she didn't even like— and never promised me anything.

What could Dad have promised her to get her to love him? And what could Mom have offered to make Dad love her back? Whatever it was, it was dying by the time I was born, and dead before I turned six. Dad could make everyone in the world smile, except Mom. And Mom was always prepared, except for what Dad did to her.

It was toward the end of February that winter, and the sun was shining and the air was crisp and clean. I sat waiting for Dad, who I knew would show up eventually.

When he got in, he was full of smiles and kisses. "Ashes!" he cried, as though it had been years since we'd last seen each other. "Have you ever seen such a day?"

I had, seven days before. But I smiled at Dad, who always seemed to discover the weather each time we visited.

"You look radiant," he said. "You get more and more beautiful. I was wearing jeans and a bulky brown sweater that Mom had given me for Christmas.

"You have flair, Ashes. Style. You're sure to make your mark."

Last week he'd told me to be an astronaut. The week before that, the CEO of a Fortune 500 corporation. And the week before that he'd been stunned by my spirituality.

"Oh, Ashes," he said, taking off his winter coat and dropping it on the sofa bed. "I wish I deserved you."

"I wouldn't have any other dad," I told him. "My friends' fathers, they just tell my friends to study more. They never tell them they have flair or style."

"Maybe they don't," Dad said. "You're the special one, Ashes. You're the one-in-a-million girl."

"Am I really?" I asked, not needing the reassurance. I knew I wasn't a one-in-a-million girl, no matter how often Dad told me I was. I still loved hearing him say it.

"One in a million," he said. "And don't let anyone ever tell you otherwise, Ashes. They will, you know. They'll try to tear you down. They'll laugh at your dreams. Even your mother— and she's a saint to have put up with me all those years—even she will discourage you from being all you can be. I hate to speak against her, but she's not a dreamer, Ashes. She's the most level-headed woman I know. As straight as a yardstick. But I was the only dream she ever believed in and once I failed her, she never let herself dream again."

We were both silent as we pondered Mom. Then Dad laughed. "She'd never let you go hungry," he said. "What do you want for supper, Ashes? I can offer you pizza, Chinese, or fast." He clapped his hands. "There's a new diner, opened right around the block. Let's treat ourselves, Ashes, and go out on the town."

"Can you afford it?" I asked.

"For a special date with my daughter?" he replied. "Of course I can afford it. Besides, I have something to celebrate."

"What?" I asked.

"I have a chance at something really big," he said. "All I need to do is put together a little financing, and I'll be set for life."

"For life?" I said, and I must have sounded like Mom because he stopped smiling.

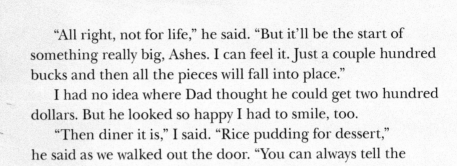

"All right, not for life," he said. "But it'll be the start of something really big, Ashes. I can feel it. Just a couple hundred bucks and then all the pieces will fall into place."

I had no idea where Dad thought he could get two hundred dollars. But he looked so happy I had to smile, too.

"Then diner it is," I said. "Rice pudding for dessert," he said as we walked out the door. "You can always tell the quality of a diner by its rice pudding."

The diner might have been brand new; but already it had a shabby, run-down quality that made it fit right in with the neighbourhood. Dad took a booth that faced the door, and sat in the seat where he could check who was coming in. He hadn't done that with me in a long time, and my stomach was hurting in an old familiar way.

"Waiting for someone?" I asked him.

"Of course not," he said. "Not when I'm with you. Take your pick, Ashes. Hamburger, triple-decker, chicken salad platter. Whatever you want."

I ordered the burger and fries, hoping that by the time it came I'd feel like eating. Dad ordered coffee.

"You'll share my fries," I said to him.

"I'll even eat your pickle," he said. But then he looked back at the door.

"What is it?" I asked him.

"It's nothing," he said. "Oh well, Ashes, you can always see right through me." He was the one who'd been looking right through me toward the door, but I didn't say anything.

"That money," he said. "The two hundred dollars?"

I nodded.

"Well it isn't so much for a deal as to help pay off one I already made," Dad said. "But I've got to tell you honey, once that money is paid, I'm on my way to easy street. Just a little setback. But you know how those guys are. They get itchy when you owe them money. And it's not always comfortable to be where they can scratch you."

"You owe them two hundred dollars?" I asked, trying to keep the panic out of my voice.

"Give or take," Dad said. "But don't worry about it, honey. I'll work it out. I always do."

My burger and fries came then. Dad took a long sip of his coffee, while I poured ketchup on my plate and twirled a fry in it. "Can I help?" I asked.

Dad smiled like I'd offered him the key to the mint. "I love you so much," he said. "You're ten thousand times better than I deserve, Ashes."

"Have a fry," I said, pushing my plate toward him. Dad took one. He seemed to have more of an appetite than I did.

"I had a thought," he said as he reached for my pickle. "Your mother keeps a couple hundred cash at her place."

I didn't think either of us was supposed to know that.

"In that pretty teapot her mother gave her," Dad said. "Unless she's changed her hiding place. I know she changed the locks, so maybe she changed her hiding place as well."

Sometimes, when Mom wasn't home, I'd take the lid off the teapot and stare into it, imagining what I could do with two hundred dollars. I looked at Dad and realized he'd had those same fantasies. Well, why not. I was his daughter, after all.

"The money's still in the teapot," I said. "What do you want to do, Dad?" I asked. "Come into the apartment with me and take the money?"

"Oh no," he said, and he looked really shocked. "I would never steal from your mother. I've caused her pain enough."

He added casually, "No, I just thought maybe you could borrow the money. Just for a day or two, until I straighten out all my finances. Your mother would never know the difference. Unless there's an earthquake or the Martians invade. I think we can gamble neither of those things will happen before Friday."

"You'll be able to pay her back by Friday?" I asked.

"You," Dad said. "I'd be borrowing the money from you. And I swear to you, Ashes, I'd have the money in your hands by Friday at the latest." He wiped his hand on the napkin and offered it to me as though to shake on the deal.

"That's a lot of money. What if Mom finds out?"

"It's me she'd be angry at," Dad said. "Which is why she'll never find out. I wouldn't jeopardize our time together, honey. You let me have the money tonight, I'll straighten out my little difficulty, and Thursday night, when your mom is out, I'll give you back what I owe you. No earthquakes, no Martians, no problem."

"Mom'll be home soon," I said.

"You all through?" he asked. I nodded. "Let's go, then," he said, the rice-pudding test long forgotten. We went back to his place so I could pick up my books. Then we walked down to his car. "Why don't you sell your car?" I asked him.

"You're your mother's daughter," he said. "Good head on your shoulders. Problem is, I'd never be able to find another car this cheap to replace it. No, Ashes, the teapot's the way to go."

We drove back to Mom's in silence. For a moment, a cloud drifted past the moon and the sky turned greenish grey.

"Snow tomorrow," Dad said. "Maybe you'll get a snow day."

"Maybe," I said.

Dad parked the car a block away from Mom's. "Just in case she gets home early," he said. "I don't want her to see me waiting. You go up to the apartment," he said. "Take the money, and come right down. Then I'll drop you off in front of her place, like always, and she'll never know the difference."

"What do I do if Mom's already there?" I asked.

"Just stay where you are," he said. "If you're not back here in ten minutes, I'll go home."

"All right," I said, and reached to unlock the door.

"You're one in a million," he said to me.

I got out of the car and ran over to the apartment. I took the elevator to the tenth floor and unlocked the door. I walked into the kitchen and turned on the light. The teapot was right where it belonged. I lifted its lid and stared at her emergency money.

Her earthquake money. Her Martian money. What should I do?

I looked out the window and saw only ash-grey sky. In the cold stillness of the night, I could hear my father's car keening in the distance. "You're one in a million," it cried.

eBook **Extra**

Responding

What Do You Think Now? "When two people argue, one person is always right." Has your response to this statement changed after reading this selection? Support your answer.

Understanding Short Stories: Writers often repeat a detail to help readers understand a story's central idea. Identify details that the writer repeats in "Ashes." How does repetition support your understanding?

Making Inferences: What did you infer from the story's final paragraph? Explain why.

Making Connections: How do you feel about how the father treats the daughter? How did your personal experiences affect your response?

Reading Like a Writer: An effective way to describe one character is to contrast that character with another. Explain how the author uses this method to develop an impression of the mother.

Critical Literacy: Imagine the story told by the father instead of the daughter. Do you think you would feel the same way toward the characters? Why or why not?

Media Literacy: If you were filming the scene in the diner, what kind of lighting and camera angles would you use? Explain why.

Metacognition: What elements of short stories did you find most helpful in understanding and responding to "Ashes"?

What do you think?

Admitting blame is a necessary part of resolving any conflict.

Strongly Disagree   Strongly Agree

1	2	3	4	5

Accident

Short Story by Dave Eggers

VOCABULARY

livid: very angry

obstructing: blocking

submerged: under water

Vocabulary Tip

Word choice is important when describing emotions. The narrator uses three adjectives when predicting the reaction of the teens: *upset*, *livid*, and *violence-contemplating*. *Livid* is stronger than *upset*, but not as extreme as *violence-contemplating*.

You all get out of your cars. You are alone in yours, and there are three teenagers in theirs, an older Camaro in new condition. The accident was your fault, and you walk over to tell them this.

Walking over to their car, which you have ruined, it occurs to you that if the three teenagers are angry teenagers, this encounter could be very unpleasant. You pulled into an intersection, obstructing them, and their car hit yours. They have every right to be upset, or livid, or even violence-contemplating.

As you approach, you see that their driver's side door won't open. The driver pushes against it, and you are reminded of scenes where drivers are stuck in submerged cars. Soon they all exit through the passenger side door and walk around the Camaro, inspecting the damage. None of them is hurt, but the car is wrecked. "Just bought this today," the driver says. He is 18, blond, average in all ways. "Today?" you ask.

You are a bad person, you think. You also think: what a dorky car for a teenager to buy in 2005. "Yeah, today," he says, then sighs. You tell him that you are sorry. That you are so, so sorry. That it was your fault and that you will cover all costs.

You exchange insurance information, and you find yourself, minute by minute, ever more thankful that none of these teenagers has punched you, or even made a remark about your being drunk, which you are not, or being stupid, which you are, often. You become more friendly with all of them, and you realize that you are much more connected to them, particularly to the driver, than possible in perhaps any other way.

You have done him and his friends harm, in a way, and you jeopardized their health, and now you are so close you feel like you share a heart. He knows your name and you know his, and you almost killed him and, because you got so close to doing so but didn't, you want to fall on him, weeping, because you are so lonely, so lonely always, and all contact is contact, and all contact makes us so grateful we want to cry and dance and cry and cry.

In a moment of clarity, you finally understand why boxers, who want so badly to hurt each other, can rest their heads on the shoulders of their opponents, can lean against one another like tired lovers, so thankful for a moment of peace.

eBook *Extra*

Responding

What Do You Think Now? "Admitting blame is a necessary part of resolving any conflict." How do you respond to this statement now that you've read "Accident"?

Analyzing Short Stories: Why do you think the author uses "you" in the way he does? How does this use affect your understanding of and response to the story?

Making Connections: Can you think of a time in your life when admitting blame helped resolve a conflict or when refusing to admit blame prolonged a conflict? Explain.

Making Inferences: What can you infer about the past of each driver? How do you know this?

Critical Literacy: Imagine the same story being told from the point of view of the teenage driver. How might this affect your response to it?

Literary Devices: How effective is the analogy the author creates to describe the first driver's reaction to the younger driver? Explain.

Evaluating: How effectively do you think the author conveyed the experience of the car accident? Support your answer with specific references to the story.

Metacognition: Were you able to put yourself in the role of the driver who caused the accident? If yes, what made it possible for you to do so? If no, what kept you from imagining yourself in this role?

How to

INTERPRET MEDIA MESSAGES

ANALYZING IMAGES

You're exposed to illustrations, photos, logos, diagrams, and other types of images every day. It's important to view images critically and understand their effect on you. When analyzing an image, ask yourself the following questions:

- What message does the image send? How do I respond to that message?

- Who created the image? Does this person or organization have special knowledge of the subject?

- For whom is the image intended? What do I know about this audience?

- For what purpose was the image created?

- What is within the frame of the image? Why is the image framed in this way?

- Is anything missing from the image? What else might have been included? Why was it left out?

- What story does the image tell?

starring
cameron CRUZ and brad CLOONEY

directed by
stephanie TARANTINO

the
accident

"A speeding race to the finish that leads to a crashing good time. Two thumbs way up! Don't miss it!"

In association with Paradown Pictures and Save-It Insurance

Your experiences and values shape your understanding of any text. Because no two people share the exact same experiences, different people may respond quite differently to the same image. How would someone who has been in an accident respond to this movie poster?

ANALYZING THE STRUCTURE OF AN IMAGE

Like written text, images have structures that help viewers/readers understand their messages. When analyzing the structure of an image, ask yourself the following questions:

- What is your eye drawn to first? How has the creator made this stand out?

- How is colour used in the image? What effect does it have on you?

- Do you notice any shapes or patterns in the arrangement of elements? If so, how do these shapes or patterns relate to the impact of the image?

- What written text is included? How effectively does the text grab your attention?

- What is the relationship among the ideas, objects, and/or people in the image? How does this relationship make you feel? How is this image linked to other images?

- What message is sent by the structure of the image? How does it match up with the message sent by the image itself?

Media Tip

When we discuss written texts, we think about how the writer uses word choice, fluency, voice, and organization to convey ideas. In the same way, when discussing the meaning of media texts, think about elements such as content, colour, organization, patterns, and use of text.

Using lighting, camera angles, and other visual techniques, photographers can manipulate viewers' interpretations of media texts. What messages do these images send?

Transfer Your Learning

Connect to ...

Technology: What technologies do you use to help you create images? How can the strategies above help you improve your use of technology to create images?

Math: How might the ability to recognize visual patterns support you in math?

What do you think?

Internal conflict is easier to cope with than external conflict.

Strongly Disagree				Strongly Agree
1	2	3	4	5

Interpreting Media Messages

To interpret any media text, consider its purpose and audience. What audience would most likely find this graphic text appealing? What is its purpose?

THE WOLVES INSIDE

Graphic Story based on a Cherokee tale
Illustrated by Chris King

A CHEROKEE ELDER SPOKE ONE DAY TO HER GRANDSON ABOUT A BATTLE OF WOLVES.

MY SON, THERE IS A BATTLE THAT GOES ON WITHIN US ALL ...

BETWEEN A WOLF CALLED EVIL...

WHO MAKES US ANGRY, GREEDY, JEALOUS, AND DECEITFUL ...

AND A WOLF CALLED GOOD...

WHO MAKES US PEACEFUL, GENEROUS, AND LOVING TOWARD OTHER HUMAN BEINGS.

BUT GRANDMOTHER, WHICH WOLF WINS THIS BATTLE?

MY SON, THE ONE YOU FEED.

Responding

What Do You Think Now? "Internal conflict is easier to cope with than external conflict." How do you feel about this statement after viewing and reading "The Wolves Inside"? Why?

Interpreting Media Messages: What message does this media text send? What elements work most effectively to send that message?

Making Inferences: What do you infer from the appearance of the figures in "The Wolves Inside"? How does this affect your understanding of the media text?

Media Literacy: If this media text was adapted to a short animated film, would you frame the action in the same way the graphic artist did? Why or why not?

Evaluating: "The Wolves Inside" is based on a Cherokee folk tale. Do you think the images are an effective adaptation of the folk tale? Support your answer with specific references to the text.

Metacognition: How does understanding the layout and structure of graphic texts affect your response to this media text?

What do you think?

What needs to be done to unite people who are in bitter conflict with each other?

ONE TEAM,

Documentary Transcript narrated by Morgan Freeman

IN ORDER OF APPEARANCE

MORGAN FREEMAN: narrator (always off-camera)

DAN RATHER: newscaster

JOHN CARLIN: journalist

MORNÉ DU PLESSIS: 1995 Springboks manager

JUSTICE BEKEBEKE: former political prisoner

NELSON MANDELA: former president of South Africa

JACOBUS FRANÇOIS PIENAAR: Springboks captain

JAMES SMALL: rugby player

HENNIE LE ROUX: rugby player

SPORTSCASTER

LINGA MOONSAMY: Nelson Mandela's former bodyguard

PAMELA GUSH: lifelong Springboks fan

ARRIE ROSSOUW: South African journalist

Opening scene: Sound of heavy metal door being shut. Sound of cheering crowd as Mandela appears.

FREEMAN: May, 1994. Four years after his release from prison, Nelson Mandela stands before his nation as South Africa's first democratically elected president. But beneath the hope surrounding his rise, the remnants of decades of apartheid are dangerously smouldering. His country, still divided, is on the brink of implosion.

RATHER: In 20 months of increased South African racial violence, more than 750 people have been killed.

CARLIN: There were an awful lot of right wingers who were threatening war, who were organizing for war.

VOCABULARY

apartheid: a policy of racial segregation in South Africa that officially ended in 1994

oppressors: people who keep other people down

Springboks: South African national rugby team

Vocabulary Tip

The term *apartheid* comes from an Afrikaans word meaning "separateness." It is pronounced "apart-hite."

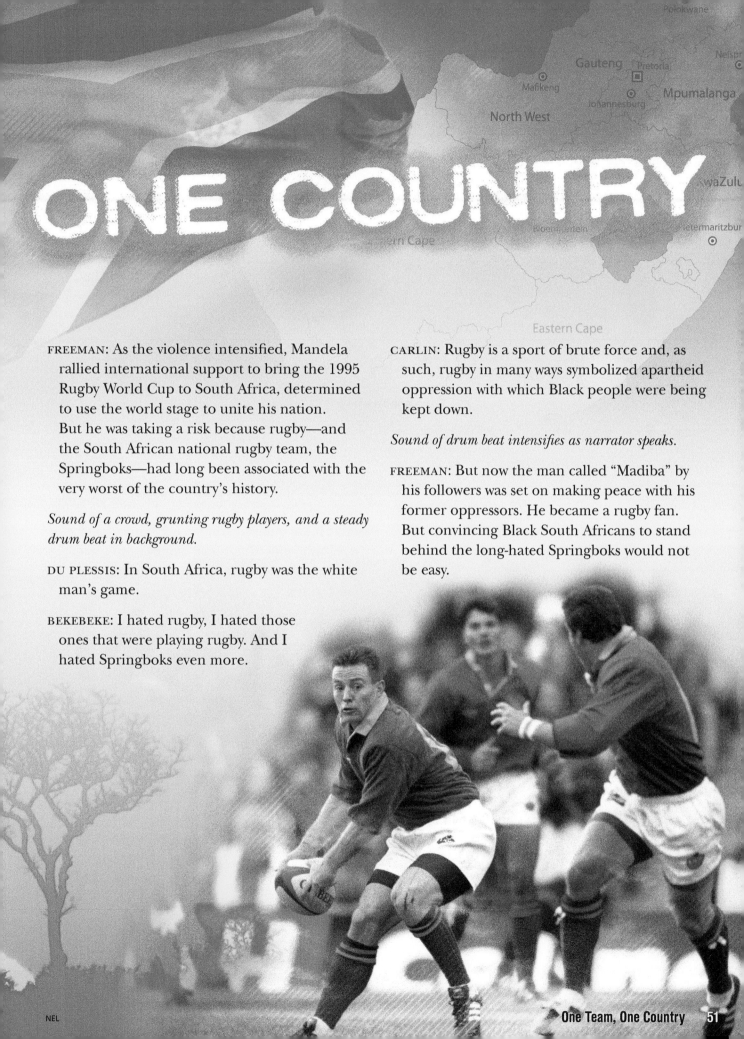

ONE COUNTRY

FREEMAN: As the violence intensified, Mandela rallied international support to bring the 1995 Rugby World Cup to South Africa, determined to use the world stage to unite his nation. But he was taking a risk because rugby—and the South African national rugby team, the Springboks—had long been associated with the very worst of the country's history.

Sound of a crowd, grunting rugby players, and a steady drum beat in background.

DU PLESSIS: In South Africa, rugby was the white man's game.

BEKEBEKE: I hated rugby, I hated those ones that were playing rugby. And I hated Springboks even more.

CARLIN: Rugby is a sport of brute force and, as such, rugby in many ways symbolized apartheid oppression with which Black people were being kept down.

Sound of drum beat intensifies as narrator speaks.

FREEMAN: But now the man called "Madiba" by his followers was set on making peace with his former oppressors. He became a rugby fan. But convincing Black South Africans to stand behind the long-hated Springboks would not be easy.

MANDELA: You see this cap that I'm wearing? I ask you all to stand behind them tomorrow because they are our pride.

Sound of crowd expressing collective disapproval of Mandela's request.

BEKEBEKE: Here is the man, wanting us to reconcile with these brutish people who have humiliated us for ages in our own country. I wasn't going to be persuaded even by the great Madiba to support the Springboks.

FREEMAN: As the World Cup approached, Mandela repeated his message of "one team, one country" in townships and villages across South Africa. Moved by Mandela's support, the Springboks players visited the Robben Island prison, where Mandela had been jailed for nearly three decades.

PIENAAR: You got into the cell and you realize he sat here for … how many years? I remember James Small standing in the corner and there were tears running down his cheeks.

SMALL: It was quite amazing to experience just for a few moments what a man experienced for a lifetime. You didn't really understand how big this whole thing was until you saw that.

LE ROUX: That also made us realize that what we were doing was a little bit more than just playing a game.

FREEMAN: The underdog Springboks, newly inspired, began a magical run through the tournament. But as the team advanced, something even more improbable happened. Black South Africans started to stand behind the national team. *One team, one country*—that was Mandela's vision. And on the morning of the final game, Blacks and whites alike were swept up into a shared frenzy of excitement. The match remains one of the epic finals in rugby history. As play headed to overtime, Mandela sat in the president's box, his great experiment hanging in the balance.

SPORTSCASTER: Yes, it's over! That is it, the final whistle and South Africa wins the Rugby World Cup Final—and what a finish for the host country!

LE ROUX: I don't think I've ever seen so many grown men on the rugby field cry.

FREEMAN: After the win, Nelson Mandela, wearing the symbol of his former enemies, stepped onto the field.

MOONSAMY: The crowd just went wild.

GUSH: It was like a volcano erupting.

Sound of crowd roaring, "Nelson! Nelson! Nelson!"

DU PLESSIS: I'm trying to understand what the chant was and I realize that these white South African people were chanting their president's name.

GUSH: "Nelson, Nelson." It was one voice.

ROSSOUW: I never thought that we would hear that at a rugby stadium. At the time, I think it was just fantastic.

SMALL: We didn't know what hit us. I mean it really was just the most phenomenal … it was really quite incredible.

Sound of gentle symphonic music as narrator speaks.

FREEMAN: The image of a joyous Mandela celebrating with the national team was mirrored in every corner of the once-broken country. South Africans, at last, were rejoicing as one.

BEKEBEKE: It was freedom all over the moment that the cup was handed over to Madiba. I told myself that these are people that have to build this country together. There's one South Africa. All my hatred is going to give me absolutely nothing.

PIENAAR: Madiba took my hand and he shook it, and he said, "Thank you very much for what you have done for South Africa." I said to him, "Madiba, you've got it wrong. Thank you for what you've done for South Africa."

BEKEBEKE: I think it was a great vision from the man to have used that opportunity to make us see each other. This is *our* South Africa.

eBook**Extra**

Responding

What Do You Think Now? "What needs to be done to unite people who are in bitter conflict with each other?" How do you respond now that you've read the selection?

Interpreting Media Messages: The documentary "One Team, One Country" is over eight minutes long. Do you think this version effectively conveys the message of the title? Why or why not?

Making Inferences: Why do you think rugby player James Small was moved to tears at Robben Island?

Evaluating: How effectively are the images in this selection linked to each other? Support your answer with specific references to the text.

Metacognition: Think of the connections you made as you read this selection. Were they primarily text to self, text to text, or text to world? Why do you think you made these kinds of connections? How did they support your reading of this text?

How to

DEVELOP AND ORGANIZE IDEAS

PREWRITING

Prewriting means using techniques to help you develop and organize ideas for your writing. Most writers use one or more of the following prewriting techniques:

- brainstorming ideas with a group
- jotting down ideas
- creating graphics, such as a concept map or plot outline

STRATEGIES FOR DEVELOPING IDEAS FOR A SHORT STORY

Develop ideas for short stories by asking these questions:

- Who is my main character?
- What do I know about that character?
- What does this character want more than anything?
- How can I keep my main character from getting what he or she wishes (at least for part of the story)? This will help you develop a problem or conflict that will add suspense to your story.

STRATEGIES FOR ORGANIZING IDEAS IN A SHORT STORY

1. Start your story with a strong lead (the first few lines) so that your readers will want to read more. Begin with action, dialogue, or thoughts about the problem or conflict.
2. Arrange the events in your story so that they build to a climax.
3. Convey information about characters and events in a variety of ways, including the thoughts of the characters, dialogue, narration, foreshadowing, and flashback. If you use a flashback, let your readers know you're going back in time.
4. Decide how you want to resolve the problem or conflict. The ending of your story must develop naturally based on what comes before it. Even stories with surprise endings include details that prepare readers to fully believe the twist when it happens.

For example, when Don Aker was writing "Scars," he developed the following plan:

Who is the main character? Daniel

What do I know about the main character? not mechanical; not getting along with father; brother just died

What does Daniel want? wants his father to accept him; wants his father to love him

How do I keep Daniel from getting what he wants? The memory of his "perfect" brother makes Daniel feel like he doesn't measure up.

Writing Poetry

To develop and organize ideas for poetry, use some of the same strategies as you do for short stories. Use the same prewriting strategies and think about the kind of poem you will write, for example, free verse, haiku, concrete poem, or limerick.

STRATEGIES FOR DEVELOPING IDEAS FOR NONFICTION TEXTS

- **Freewrite** for three to five minutes about topics or events you feel strongly about (for example, the environment or your favourite band).

- Decide if your **topic is focused** enough to explore in a single piece of writing. A broad topic, such as the environment, could lead in different directions.

- **Use a graphic** to help you narrow your topic.

- **Write about what you know and care about.** If you choose to write about a topic you don't know well, make sure you do your research.

environment

extreme environments → ocean depths → Marianas Trench

conservation → green initiatives → composting

careers → biologist → marine biologist

Here's how one student has narrowed her topic from "the environment" to "Marianas Trench."

STRATEGIES FOR ORGANIZING IDEAS IN NONFICTION TEXTS

Establish your **purpose and audience** before beginning your writing. Often your **purpose will suggest a way to organize** your writing. Below are some examples of matching purpose and organization. Feel free to experiment.

PURPOSE	POSSIBLE ORGANIZATION
to explain a process	Arrange the parts of the process in a sequence that readers can easily follow (for example, time order), and explain each part in detail.
to explain the cause of an event	Describe the event and then examine each of its causes, or present the causes and then describe the event that resulted from them.
to persuade readers to follow some course of action	Present your thesis (main idea) in the first paragraph. Support your thesis in the following paragraphs presenting your most compelling argument last. Your concluding paragraph should summarize the arguments and repeat the thesis.
to compare two things or ideas	Discuss their similarities and then discuss their differences.

Transfer Your Learning

Connect to ...

Media Literacy: Compare the process of developing and organizing ideas while writing to the same process when creating media texts.

Technology: How can you use search engines to help you narrow your topic before you start researching or writing?

Reading Like a Writer

▶ Developing and Organizing Ideas

Developing Ideas

A topic must be narrow enough so that a writer can explore it fully in a single piece of writing. Do you think this topic will be narrow enough? Explain.

VOCABULARY

fervently: strongly or intensely

pungent: with a strong smell or taste

unionized: organized in a labour union

Vocabulary Tip

Look at the parts of a word to help you figure out its meaning. For example, *unionized* has the root word *union*, so you can figure out this word is connected with labour unions.

Organizing Ideas

One way to organize a persuasive piece is to present the problem and then offer reasons why your readers should do what you suggest. As you read, think about the problem identified in this article.

What do you think?

Conflict can't be resolved without each side respecting the other.

Strongly Disagree				Strongly Agree
1	2	3	4	5

TEEN ON STRIKE

Newspaper Article by Tamie Dolny

I'm supposed to be working as a lifeguard and swimming instructor this summer at Etobicoke's Memorial Pool. Instead, as a member of CUPE Local 79, I'm on strike. And on Canada Day, I picketed at the Ingram Transfer Station.

I've never really spent time with a group of men. Boys, certainly, but not honest-to-goodness men. And to tell you the truth, they're not that different—just bigger, smellier, hairier, taller, and wider. During a strike, they're also incredibly interesting.

How could Canada Day be boring when your mother drives you to a dump site in the middle of nowhere, smiles and waves at you, and then drives away, screeching her tires?

Just 16, I was left to fend for myself in the testosterone jungle of picketing members of CUPE Locals 79 and 416.

Ingram Transfer Station, I learned, is code for a dump-and-run garbage zone where peeved-off unemployed workers stand around and burn stuff. It was the most potentially dangerous situation I'd ever been in at seven in the morning. Tall, ferocious-looking unionized garbage workers and office staff stood around amid piles of rotting trash. There was nobody, aside from me, under the age of 25. So I set myself down on a curb, rested my head in my hands, and glared at everyone in that I-am-a-spoiled-teenager-and-I-don't-want-to-be-here fashion.

Little did I know how much I would learn.

I'm not your typical city worker. As a teenager, I fervently practise three activities: staying up too late, talking back to my parents, and giggling about boys. Going on strike was not part of my summer plans.

I started off not caring at all about the actual meaning of the dispute: I was there for the strike pay, not to support my fellow workers. If I worked for just four hours a day, five days a week, CUPE 79 would pay me $200. For a student like me, that seems like decent enough money. I soon got a reality check.

I am currently scheduled at the York Civic Centre, where I picket in the back parking lot. On my first day, a woman brought along her two-year-old toddler, for whom she couldn't find daycare. The second day, I overheard another woman talking about being behind on her phone bill.

We've been striking for nearly four weeks now: $200 times four equals $800, right?

In an expensive city like Toronto, $800 barely manages to cover rent, if you're lucky. On top of that are food, clothes, utility bills, and miscellaneous needs and desires. Some people live from paycheque to paycheque. A strike could cost them their home and credit rating.

Organizing Ideas

Writers of persuasive pieces must have a strong sense of the audience they are trying to convince. Do you think Tamie Dolny understands her audience? Has she arranged her ideas with her audience in mind? Explain.

You might wonder, "Why are you on strike? And why should I care?" Well, first, when your parents tell you to go on picket duty instead of sitting around watching TV, as a dependent child, you tend to do what you're told. It's particularly ironic because my father is a manager for the City of Toronto. Imagine our dinner conversations.

And why should you care? Because it's so incredibly, mind-bogglingly unfair. The public isn't on our side. Most of the summer workers like me aren't even on our side.

I know that, and all unionized workers know that. But stay with me.

Under their current contract, which expires next year, Toronto police get a pay raise of at least 3 percent each year, and had to make no concessions. Toronto firefighters got an increase of 3 percent annually with no concessions. TTC workers got 3 percent with no concessions. Toronto Housing workers got 3 percent with no concessions. Even city councillors got a pay raise of 2.4 percent while still arguing that the city cannot afford any more union pay raises.

When initially discussing our contract with David Miller, Local 79 president Ann Dembinski reported back to the union that the city was offering something along the lines of a 0 percent raise in the first year and a 1 percent raise in the second year. As workers, we could lose money that first year because of inflation. That's pretty vile.

Back at Ingram Transfer Station, I was soon forgotten in the maze of litter and trash bags and overwhelming stench of garbage. So I continued sitting, nearly getting my feet squished by cars playing loud music, the drivers eager to drop off their stinky secrets.

Lying low turned out to be a good idea, since by that point two fights had nearly broken out between garbage dumpers and strikers, due to the overpowering scent of maleness and that crazy, I-am-tougher-and-more-macho-than-you emotion in the air.

Even so, in most of the cases when verbal fights did break out, they were started by people impatient about waiting an extra 15 minutes to dump their trash because of the picket. (When I was at Ingram, nobody waited for more than half an hour to drop off three bags of garbage.) When one guy hissed in the face of a striker, the striker hurled insults back at him. But, if certain media had been present, the striker's behaviour would probably have been described as "unprovoked," right?

I can barely claim to understand the complexities of the labour dispute. However, I can say that it's mean and hurtful when a man parks his car and grinds his wheels against the pavement, releasing pungent fumes and causing the pregnant woman who was picketing with me to start coughing.

I can say that it's insulting and degrading when a patron decides to drive through the crowd of strikers, nearly bowling us all over. I can especially say that it's so, so painfully wrong to be malicious, rude, and spiteful to a group of people who just want to make a point for 15 minutes of your day.

I'm just pleading for a bit of respect, really. You don't need to agree with what the unions are fighting for. All you need to do is grant us the basic dignity any human being deserves. Don't get angry. You'll get to where you need to go … just a couple of minutes later, that's all.

↙ Developing Ideas

Writers write best when they are passionate about the subject. What words does Tamie use to indicate she feels strongly about her subject?

eBook Extra

Responding

What Do You Think Now? "Conflict can't be resolved without each side respecting the other." Now that you've read the newspaper article, how important do you think mutual respect is in resolving conflict? Why?

Developing Ideas: Why do you suppose Tamie chose to write about the strike? How might knowing this help you generate your own ideas for writing an article?

Organizing Ideas: If Tamie was to rewrite this article to explain to readers the daily routine of a striker, how might she organize her ideas differently? What different or additional information might she provide?

Making Connections: Tamie is much younger than her co-workers. Have you ever been in a similar situation? How does making this connection support your reading?

Critical Literacy: On page 56, Tamie risks offending not only her co-workers but all male readers when she describes the men she works with as being not much different than boys, "just bigger, smellier, hairier, taller, and wider." Why do you think she takes this risk? Do you think the risk is worth it? Explain.

Media Literacy: What impact do the photos have on you? Do they support your understanding? Explain why or why not.

Evaluating: Do you think Tamie made readers feel differently toward the strikers? Why or why not?

Metacognition: Which do you prefer: developing ideas for writing fiction or nonfiction? Why? What do you think you need to do to become more comfortable developing ideas for the form you're less comfortable with?

APPLYING
WRITING
STRATEGIES

Reading Like a Writer

▶ Developing and
Organizing Ideas

What do you think?

When a country is at war, all its citizens who are able to fight should be prepared to do so.

Strongly Disagree				Strongly Agree
1	2	3	4	5

DULCE ET DECORUM EST

Poem by Wilfred Owen

VOCABULARY

ardent: very enthusiastic or passionate

flound'ring: short for *floundering*, moving clumsily and in confusion

lime: a white, chalky substance that burns the skin; lime was used in World War I to aid in the decomposition of bodies

knock-kneed: with legs curved inward so that the knees tend to touch when walking

Vocabulary Tip

Sometimes words create vivid visual images. In the case of *knock-kneed*, visualize the soldier's knees knocking together as he walks.

Bent double, like old beggars under sacks,
Knock-kneed, coughing like hags, we cursed through sludge,
Till on the haunting flares we turned our backs,
And towards our distant rest began to trudge.
Men marched asleep. Many had lost their boots,
But limped on, blood-shod. All went lame, all blind;
Drunk with fatigue; deaf even to the hoots
Of gas-shells dropping softly behind.

Gas! *Gas!* Quick, boys!—An ecstasy of fumbling
Fitting the clumsy helmets just in time,
But someone still was yelling out and stumbling
And flound'ring like a man in fire or lime.—
Dim through the misty panes and thick green light,
As under a green sea, I saw him drowning.

In all my dreams before my helpless sight
He plunges at me, guttering, choking, drowning.

If in some smothering dreams, you too could pace
Behind the wagon that we flung him in,
And watch the white eyes writhing in his face,
His hanging face, like a devil's sick of sin,
If you could hear, at every jolt, the blood
Come gargling from the froth-corrupted lungs
Bitter as the cud
Of vile, incurable sores on innocent tongues,—
My friend, you would not tell with such high zest
To children ardent for some desperate glory,
The old Lie: Dulce et decorum est
Pro patria mori.

Fallen soldier brought home from Afghanistan

Dulce et decorum est is Latin for "It is a sweet and fitting thing," the first part of a statement that is completed in the last line of the poem, "*pro patria mori*," which means "To die for your country." The lines are originally from a poem by Horace, a Roman poet from the first century BCE. The British poet Wilfred Owen (1893–1918) was killed in action one week before the end of World War I.

eBook Extra

Responding

What Do You Think Now? "When a country is at war, all its citizens who are able to fight should be prepared to do so." How do you feel about this statement after reading the poem? Explain.

Developing Ideas: How do you think the poet's personal experience in the war helped him to generate ideas for this poem? Support your answer.

Organizing Ideas: Explain why the poet organized the poem with the shortest stanza, only two lines, in the centre of the poem.

Making Connections: What text-to-text or text-to-world connections did you make as you read the selection? How did they help you understand the poem?

Critical Literacy: How do you think a soldier who has experienced a tour of duty in Afghanistan would respond to this poem? Why?

Evaluating: This poem may be read as persuasive text. How effective is the poet's argument? Explain.

Metacognition: Did you read the explanation of the title before reading the poem? Do you think the poem would have had greater or lesser impact if you had done the opposite? Explain.

How to

USE ACTIVE LISTENING STRATEGIES

To be an effective listener, you need to use active listening strategies. Active listening strategies, like the ones below, will help you understand and take meaningful notes in any listening situation (such as your classroom, a formal assembly, or a brainstorming session with your peers).

- Consider your prior knowledge. What do you expect the speaker to tell you that you don't already know?
- Make connections to help you focus on the speaker's message and to assess the speaker's accuracy.
- Identify the speaker's purpose. This may be stated directly or indirectly.
- Pay attention to the speaker's body language and facial expressions.
- Note the speaker's tone of voice.
- Pay attention to verbal or visual cues that indicate the speaker is moving from one key point to another.
- Pay attention to what is *not* said. Has the speaker left out important information? Is the speaker biased in any way?
- If possible, ask for clarification or for further information if you are unsure of the speaker's meaning.

Note-Taking Tips

- Jot down key words and ideas in point form.
- Use your own "shorthand" (for example, abbreviations or symbols).
- Sketch important ideas in simple diagrams (for example, a timeline or flow chart).
- Leave room on the page to add more details later.
- After the presentation, review your notes to see if you've omitted anything important.

When he finishes talking, I'll ask him to explain that point.

USE APPROPRIATE VOCAL STRATEGIES

To be an effective speaker, you need to develop vocal strategies that are appropriate to your purpose and audience. This means being aware of the different vocal elements and how you can use them for maximum impact.

VOCAL ELEMENT	VOCAL STRATEGY	AUDIENCE IMPACT
volume	Adjust the volume of your voice to match the size of your audience and presentation space.	To understand your message, the audience must be able to hear you clearly. Project your voice for large groups and speak more softly for smaller groups.
tone	Use a tone of voice that is appropriate for your purpose.	Your tone should help your audience appreciate the seriousness of—or humour in—your subject. In a dramatic performance, your tone should help convey a strong impression of the character.
pitch	Vary the intensity of your voice to emphasize key points.	An audience loses interest quickly when listening to a monotone voice. Varying the pitch of your voice adds interest to your presentation and importance to your ideas.
pacing	Insert pauses for emphasis.	Pauses create drama. Silence at the appropriate times gives an audience the chance to process information, as well as allowing you a brief rest before continuing.

THINK POSITIVELY

When you speak in front of a group, think positively about your audience. Most audience members genuinely want to learn what the speaker has to share.

Transfer Your Learning

Connect to ...

Media Literacy: When you're listening to dialogue in a movie, which of the active listening strategies on page 62 do you find most helpful? Why?

Careers: Think about your dream job. Do people working in that area rely on the use of appropriate vocal strategies? Explain.

► Use Active Listening Strategies

► Use Appropriate Vocal Strategies

VOCABULARY

downstage right: at or toward the front of a stage, to the audience's left

fetal position: curled up like a baby in the womb

upstage left: at or toward the back of a stage, to the audience's right

Vocabulary Tip

The terms *downstage right* and *upstage left* are examples of everyday words that are given new meaning when used as jargon. *Jargon* is specialized language used in a specific field.

Use Appropriate Vocal Strategies

→

Effective speakers pace themselves, using pauses for maximum effect on their listeners. After reading this and the Narrator's other lines, how would you pace your delivery of the lines? Explain.

What do you think?

Life is dull without conflict.

Strongly Disagree				Strongly Agree
1	2	3	4	5

Conflict

Play Excerpt by Wade Bradford

CHARACTERS
NARRATOR (male or female)
PROTAGONIST (male)
WOMAN

SETTING
A blank stage

COSTUMES
Doesn't matter

Curtains rise: The Narrator stands downstage right. Upstage left, a man—the Protagonist—lies on the floor, curled up in a fetal position.

NARRATOR: A story begins.

Lights come up on Protagonist.

NARRATOR: A child is born.

Protag (as we shall now call him) stretches, cries like a newborn baby.

NARRATOR: He grows into a man.

Protag quickly "grows" and assumes a manly pose.

BIRTH   GROWING UP   ADULTHOOD   MARRIAGE

NARRATOR: He experiences happiness.

PROTAG: *(very happy)* Ah!

NARRATOR: He experiences sadness.

PROTAG: *(very sad)* Aw …

NARRATOR: He meets a girl.

Woman approaches Protag.

PROTAG: Hello!

WOMAN: Hello.

NARRATOR: They fall in love. They get married. They go on their honeymoon.

NARRATOR: They have four children.

From somewhere offstage, an unseen cast member tosses four baby dolls. Protag lovingly catches them one after another. He drops the fourth one.

NARRATOR: Three children.

Protag and Woman lean against each other, adoring their children.

← **Use Active Listening Strategies**

Paying attention to a speaker's body language helps you understand what that person is thinking and feeling. What body language would you recommend the actor use here as he delivers this line? Explain your recommendation.

HAVING CHILDREN

MIDDLE AGE

DIVORCE

Use Appropriate Vocal Strategies ↘

Effective speakers use tone of voice to highlight key ideas or convey specific impressions. What tone do you think this statement requires? Why?

Use Active Listening Strategies ↗

Effective listeners pay attention not only to what is being said but also to what is *not* being said. What do you think is not being said here? What makes you think so?

NARRATOR: The children grow up and move away.

PROTAG: *(tossing the babies back to cast member)* G'bye kids. Good luck with college!

NARRATOR: There's a fifty-fifty chance that he and his wife divorce.

Woman flips a coin. She looks at it. Shrugs at Protag and then leaves.

NARRATOR: All alone, the man grows old.

Protag sags a little.

NARRATOR: Older …

Protag hunches over, waddling about like a very old man.

NARRATOR: Ollllderrr … and dies.

Protag falls over, lifeless.

NARRATOR: The end.

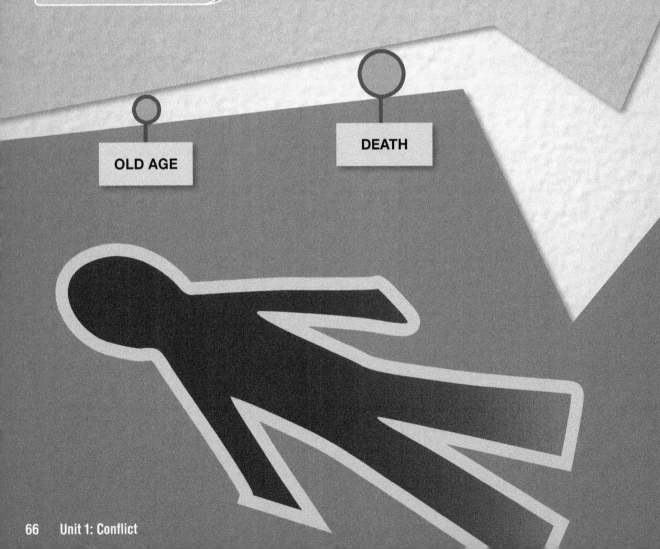

OLD AGE

DEATH

The Narrator lifts up Protag's wrist and lets it drop down to the floor.

NARRATOR: Not very satisfying, is it? And why? The story had no conflict. Conflict is a struggle, a quest, a battle, a challenge, a longing, an agony, a goal that seems forever out of our grasp. We, as an audience, desire, nay, we demand that our characters experience conflict.

As the Narrator speaks, he stands the Protag back up, and arranges him as if working with a sculpture or a mannequin.

NARRATOR: And why do we crave conflict and hardship for our main character? Why must he endure emotional and sometimes physical trial? Because each of us can relate to it. Here stands a man, but he cannot become a hero until I, the narrator, give him conflict. We need something besides the protagonist on stage. We need something … an object, a situation, or a person, that will elicit feelings, emotions, desires, and ultimately conflict.

Use Appropriate Vocal Strategies

Effective speakers vary the pitch, or intensity, of their voices to emphasize key points. Read this speech by the Narrator aloud twice. What words or phrases would you emphasize using pitch? Why?

Use Active Listening Strategies

Effective listeners make connections between what the speaker is saying and their own prior knowledge and experience. What connections can you make with the Narrator's comments here? Why is that so?

eBook*Extra*

Responding

What Do You Think Now? "Life is dull without conflict." How do you respond to this statement now that you've read the selection? Why?

Using Active Listening Strategies: If Protag were listening actively to what the Narrator was saying, which of the strategies listed on page 62 would he find most helpful? Explain.

Using Appropriate Vocal Strategies: If you were the Narrator in this play, what tone of voice would you use? Provide your reasons for using this tone.

Making Inferences: This is a brief excerpt from a longer script. Based on what you have read, what do you suppose happens in the remainder of the play? Why do you predict the play will develop in this way?

Reading Like a Writer: Why do you suppose the playwright chose not to give his characters proper names? Would the use of proper names have decreased or increased the impact of the play on you? Explain.

Media Literacy: The playwright states for costume design that it "Doesn't matter." If you were to film this selection, how would you dress the three characters? Explain your choices.

Evaluating: How effectively do you think the playwright has dealt with the importance of conflict? Support your answer with specific references to the text.

Metacognition: In what ways do you read a script differently than you do a short story? Explain.

What Do You Think Now?

THINK BACK TO YOUR ORIGINAL RESPONSE TO THIS STATEMENT: "TO BE HUMAN IS TO EXPERIENCE CONFLICT."

How have your feelings about this statement changed since you began this unit?

DEMONSTRATE YOUR LEARNING

Reflect on

- the texts you have read, viewed, and discussed during this unit
- the skills and strategies you have been developing

Select one of the following tasks to demonstrate your achievement of this unit's learning goals.

WRITE A SHORT STORY

Write a short story about a character who arrives at a better understanding of him- or herself as a result of conflict. Be sure to

- ☑ include your main character's thoughts, feelings, actions, and words
- ☑ decide what your main character wants, and how you will make it difficult or impossible for that to happen through internal and/or external conflict
- ☑ determine what will change during the course of your story
- ☑ consider how you might use symbolism, analogy, flashback, or foreshadowing

PERFORM A SCENE

For one of the selections in this unit, create and perform a scene. Be sure to

- ☑ convey a strong sense of the characters and conflict using verbal cues and body language
- ☑ use vocal strategies appropriate to your purpose and audience

CREATE A MEDIA TEXT

Choose two of the conflicts included in selections in this unit, one external and one internal. Develop a media text for each that illustrates your understanding of that conflict. For each,

- ☑ choose or create images that effectively show the conflict
- ☑ use the media elements (colour, shapes, organization, patterns, and use of text) effectively to convey your message
- ☑ develop accompanying print text suitable for an audience that has not read the selection

What's the Big Idea?

What do *you* think?

Human innovation improves lives.

Strongly Disagree				Strongly Agree
1	2	3	4	5

Unit Learning Goals

- determining main ideas
- summarizing
- identifying the elements of a biography
- developing and organizing ideas
- analyzing codes, conventions, and techniques
- using oral and visual cues to interpret text
- using interpersonal speaking skills

What's the Big Idea?

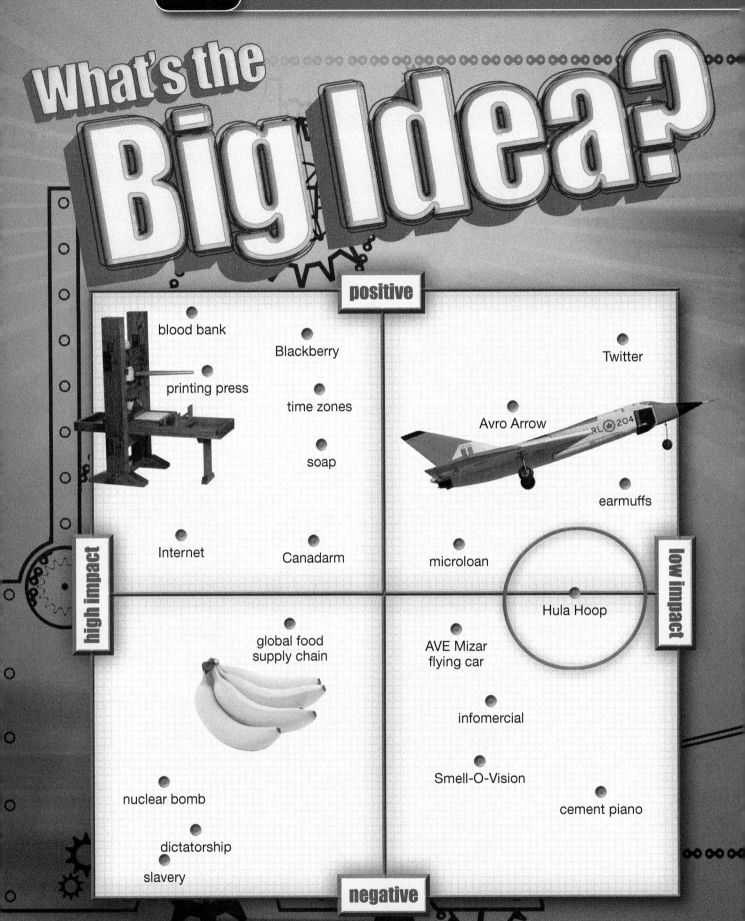

positive

blood bank

Blackberry

printing press

time zones

soap

Twitter

Avro Arrow

RL 204

earmuffs

Internet

Canadarm

microloan

high impact

low impact

Hula Hoop

global food supply chain

AVE Mizar flying car

infomercial

nuclear bomb

Smell-O-Vision

cement piano

dictatorship

slavery

negative

Human-Like Robots Unveiled

Building socially intelligent machine is just around the corner for Professor Cynthia Breazeal and MIT team

Grow Your Own Tissue with Nano-Scaffolding

Frank Ko at University of British Columbia researches human tissue regeneration

Sounds of Hope

Inspired by her family, Kayla Cornale develops teaching system that allows autistic children to learn through music

"Never doubt that a small group of thoughtful, committed citizens can change the world. Indeed, it is the only thing that ever has."

—Margaret Mead

"We can't solve problems by using the same kind of thinking we used when we created them."

—Albert Einstein

Innovation is the ability to see change as an opportunity—not a threat.

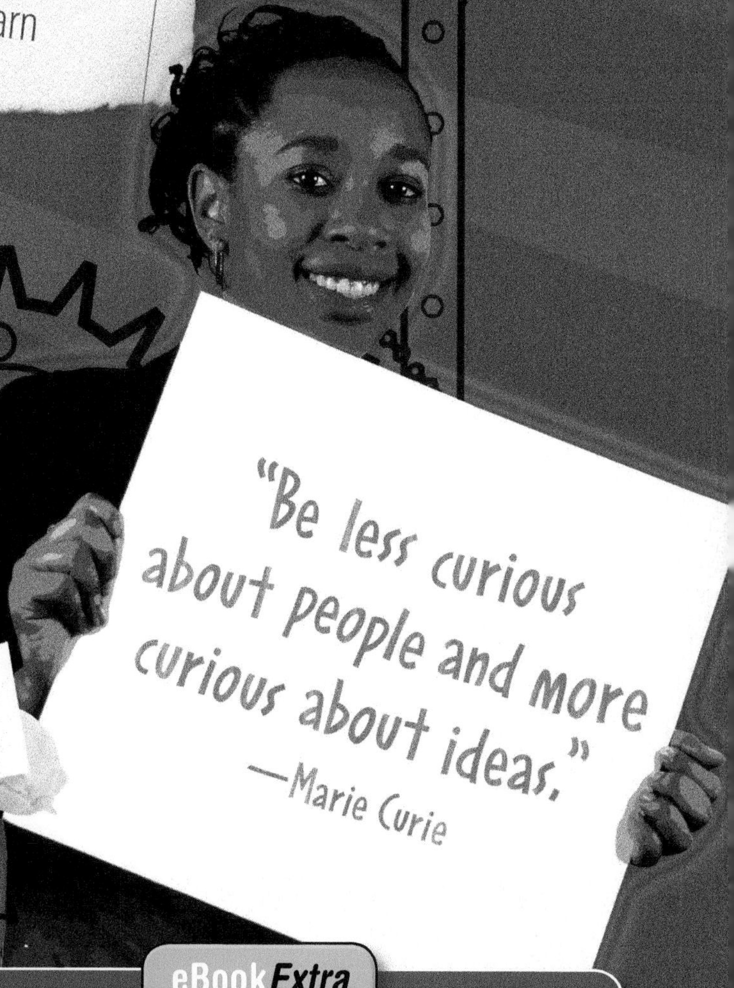

"Be less curious about people and more curious about ideas."

—Marie Curie

How to

DETERMINE MAIN IDEAS AND SUMMARIZE

Summarizing is a strategy you use all the time as you read. For example, you summarize the text when you identify the main idea. A summary is a shorter version of a longer text that focuses on the main idea. Summarizing demonstrates your understanding of a text.

Reading Tips

To help you determine which information in a text is important, pay attention to

- titles and headings
- bold, italic, or highlighted words
- phrases such as *most important, on the other hand*, and *in conclusion*
- information in diagrams, charts, or other graphics

identify a writer's message

recall important ideas

organize my thoughts

Summarizing helps me ...

identify the ideas that support a message

distinguish between important and unimportant information

STEPS TO HELP YOU DETERMINE MAIN IDEAS AND SUMMARIZE

1. READ THE ENTIRE TEXT

- Determine if the text is fiction or nonfiction.
- Determine if the text needs to be summarized in sections or as a whole.
- Determine the broad topic of the text. For example, a broad topic might be Canadian innovations of the 19th century.

2. IDENTIFY IMPORTANT INFORMATION OR KEY POINTS

Use headings, subheadings, or bolded words to help you identify key points. Summarize each section in one sentence.

3. DETERMINE THE MAIN IDEA

Determine how the key points you identified in each section relate to each other. What main idea do they reveal about the topic? For example, if the broad topic is Canadian innovations of the 19th century, the main idea might be how Canadian innovators were driven by climate and geography to find communication and transportation solutions.

4. ORGANIZE YOUR IDEAS

You can use a graphic organizer to help you summarize. For example, one of the graphic organizers below can be used to help you summarize an article that has a cause-and-effect text pattern. As well, understanding the text pattern can help you determine which information in a text is important.

Summarizing Tips

- Don't add personal opinions.

- Don't add information not in the original text.

- Summarize rather than give a table of contents.

Follow these steps when you need to create a *written* summary of a text:

- State the main idea of the text.

- Express supporting details in simple and clear language.

- Restate any conclusions.

- Use your own words.

Transfer Your Learning

Connect to …

Math: Although math problems are usually short, you need to recognize their main ideas and important details. What strategies do you use to locate main ideas in math word problems?

Exams: Many exams require you to read lengthy texts and then answer questions. Explain how summarizing the text can help you answer the questions more effectively.

Determining Main Ideas

Knowing the broad topic of a text will help you to determine the main idea. What information is revealed in the introductory section that helps you identify the topic? State the topic in a concise sentence.

VOCABULARY

attributed: gave credit for something to a particular person or group

fascism: any movement, ideology, or attitude that favours dictatorial government, centralized control of private enterprise, repression of all opposition, and extreme nationalism

maimed: inflicted a severe and permanent injury (on a person or animal)

Vocabulary Tip

The suffix *-ism* is often added to word roots to describe a doctrine, system, or principle, for example, *fascism*, *socialism*, *capitalism*, *racism*, and *multiculturalism*.

What do you think?

The greatest invention of all time is the alphabet.

Strongly Disagree				Strongly Agree
1	2	3	4	5

BIG IDEAS

Article by Elizabeth MacLeod

It's hard to imagine a world without writing, but that's an example of a really big idea that had to develop. Various cultures came up with the big idea of writing. Canadians generally use an alphabet that evolved from ancient Egyptian hieroglyphs dating around 2000 BCE. The number system we use is based on the Hindu-Arabic numerals developed in India around 500 BCE. Not only were letters and numbers big ideas, they were great ideas that spread across the world and changed our lives.

Big ideas are extremely valuable because their scope is unpredictable. It's easy to predict what kind of people have big ideas. Innovative people believe that customs and processes can be changed for the better. They're willing to work diligently to put their ideas into action. Most importantly, "big-ideas" people don't lose their hope that the world can be altered.

Not all cultures used alphabetic writing systems. Some used symbols or pictographs to communicate.

Sometimes big ideas come from coincidences and lucky breaks. Coincidence was how both potato chips and ice cream cones were invented.

Some people even say incredible leaps in invention must have a supernatural basis. For example, did the Egyptian pyramid builders really move massive blocks with simple machines and human power? Or did they receive directions and help from aliens or time travellers?

On the other hand, most people would argue that big ideas and innovations come from hard work over a long period of time—from testing and retesting your ideas until you get them right.

HARD WORK AND MOTIVATION

People who have big ideas and then make something out of them are willing to work hard and are persistent. That's how a cash-strapped teacher of deaf children changed how the world communicates. Alexander Graham Bell spent long nights working in his lab to invent the telephone. He refused to give up and was rewarded with a place in history.

Marie Curie is famous for her work with radiation. It took many years for her to prove her theories about radioactive material. Marie's determination helped make radiation a treatment to kill cancer cells.

George Washington Carver believed that things could be different for poor Black farmers living in the southern United States in the early 1900s. If they could improve their soil, they could grow better crops and make more money. George knew that growing peanuts could improve soil conditions. So he didn't stop working until he had invented more than 325 peanut products. Peanut butter was one of those products.

For 45 years, Jane Goodall studied the social and family interactions of chimpanzees. Her most groundbreaking discovery was that chimps make tools—something previously only attributed to humans. She also established the Jane Goodall Institute and the Roots & Shoots youth group. As a result, she is recognized as a global leader in protecting chimps and their habitat.

Marie Curie won many top science awards.

Determining Main Ideas and Summarizing

Distinguishing between important and less important information is key when determining main points. In this section of the text, what information do you consider important? Unimportant? State what is important in one concise sentence.

Mushroom clouds, such as this one, are associated with nuclear bombs and the massive destruction they cause.

WHEN GOOD IDEAS GO BAD

It's obvious that big ideas such as slavery or fascism are also bad ideas. Clearly, big ideas are not always good ideas. The United States ended World War II when it dropped nuclear bombs on two cities in Japan. Ending a major war was obviously a good idea. However, hundreds of thousands of Japanese people were killed or maimed. Most people agree that nuclear bombs = bad idea!

The global food supply chain is a fairly simple idea. We can grow, make, or package food wherever we want and send it to whomever wants it. Strawberries all year? Sounds great! The environmental impact alone makes this a bad idea. Large crops for global supply mean large amounts of pesticides and lots of travel time. After they are picked, strawberries are shipped via train, truck, and other vehicles that rely on fossil fuels.

LITTLE BIG IDEAS

Sometimes ideas to solve big problems start small and then grow. For instance, have you followed anyone on Twitter today? This social networking service started as a way for employees at one podcasting company to communicate. Now it's a worldwide phenomenon with one of the fastest-growing websites.

Microloans are small amounts of money that are lent to people who otherwise would never qualify to start businesses. They help poor people get employment or begin employing others. This little idea began in Pakistan and has spread around the world.

This sculpture of a thinker is one of the best known sculptures in the world. Is it because we respect people who come up with great ideas? Especially if they make lots of money? Is Bill Gates a more respected thinker than Confucius?

BIG IDEAS THAT HELP OTHERS

Everyone knows about Terry Fox and his attempt to run across Canada to raise money for cancer research. He originally hoped to bring in just $1 million, but Marathon of Hope events have since raised more than $400 million.

Mother Teresa had a big idea—and became an international advocate for the poor and helpless; through her efforts, one mission in India expanded to over 600 around the world.

RIGHT PLACE, RIGHT TIME

Anyone can have a world-changing idea. Sometimes it just takes being in the right place at the right time. And there's no way of predicting that unique place or time. Will you have the next big idea?

Many girls in Afghanistan don't have the opportunity to go to school. When 9-year-old Alaina Podmorrow heard about this, her big idea was to start the charity Little Women for Little Women, which helps Afghan girls go to school.

eBook *Extra*

Responding

What Do You Think Now? In your opinion, what is the greatest invention of all time? How did reading this selection influence your answer?

Determining Main Ideas: When determining main ideas in this text, did you find it difficult to distinguish between important and unimportant information? Explain. What strategies helped you with this challenge?

Summarizing: Write a concise summary of this text. Be sure to state the main idea, key supporting details, and any conclusions drawn by the author. Use your own words.

Drawing Conclusions: Can anyone come up with a big idea? What characteristics do people with big ideas possess?

Critical Literacy: Who might feel left out by this article? Why?

Metacognition: How does determining main ideas and summarizing a text help you increase your understanding of it? What specific strategies did you find most useful?

VOCABULARY

diodes: devices through which electric current can pass freely in only one direction

hypertext: a collection of documents containing cross-references, or "links," which, with the aid of an interactive browser program, allow readers to move easily from one document to another

perceptible: capable of being perceived; recognizable; appreciable

Vocabulary Tip
Sometimes knowing another form of a word can help you guess its meaning. The word *perceptible* is related to *perceive* and *perception*. Since *perception* involves "seeing," then something that is *perceptible* can be seen or recognized.

What do you think?
The most important technological innovation in your life is …

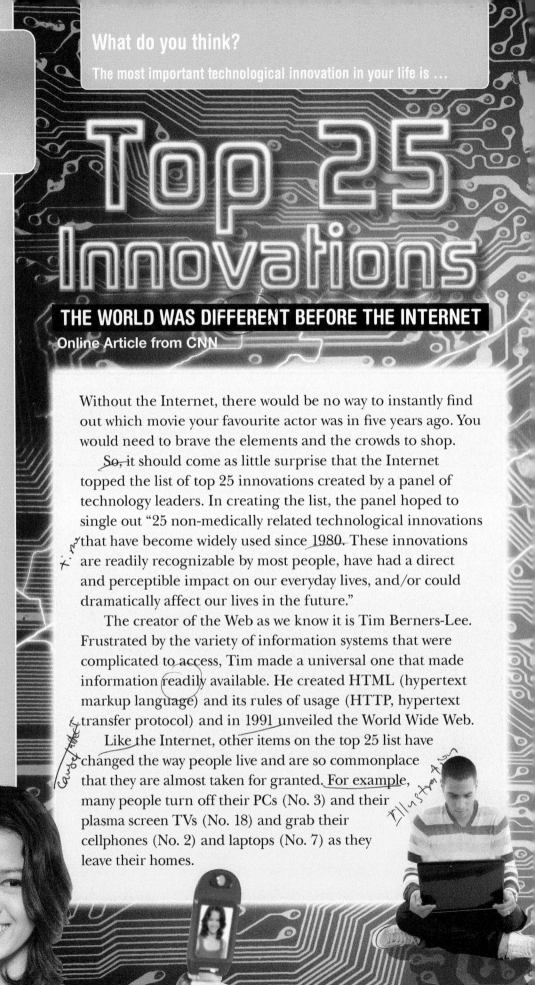

Top 25 Innovations

THE WORLD WAS DIFFERENT BEFORE THE INTERNET
Online Article from CNN

Without the Internet, there would be no way to instantly find out which movie your favourite actor was in five years ago. You would need to brave the elements and the crowds to shop.

So, it should come as little surprise that the Internet topped the list of top 25 innovations created by a panel of technology leaders. In creating the list, the panel hoped to single out "25 non-medically related technological innovations that have become widely used since 1980. These innovations are readily recognizable by most people, have had a direct and perceptible impact on our everyday lives, and/or could dramatically affect our lives in the future."

The creator of the Web as we know it is Tim Berners-Lee. Frustrated by the variety of information systems that were complicated to access, Tim made a universal one that made information readily available. He created HTML (hypertext markup language) and its rules of usage (HTTP, hypertext transfer protocol) and in 1991 unveiled the World Wide Web.

Like the Internet, other items on the top 25 list have changed the way people live and are so commonplace that they are almost taken for granted. For example, many people turn off their PCs (No. 3) and their plasma screen TVs (No. 18) and grab their cellphones (No. 2) and laptops (No. 7) as they leave their homes.

1. the Internet
2. cellphones
3. personal computers
4. fibre optics
5. e-mail
6. commercialized GPS
7. portable computers
8. memory-storage discs
9. consumer-level digital cameras
10. radio-frequency ID tags
11. microelectromechanical system (MEMS)
12. DNA fingerprinting
13. airbags
14. ATMs
15. advanced batteries
16. hybrid cars
17. organic light-emitting diodes (OLEDs)
18. display panels
19. HDTV
20. the space shuttle
21. nanotechnology
22. flash memory
23. voice mail
24. modern hearing aids
25. short-range, high-frequency radio

Some check their e-mail (No. 5) via short-range high-frequency radio (WI-FI, No. 25) and their voice mail (No. 23), before heading off to an ATM (No. 14) for cash.

The technology that makes these items possible is taken even more for granted by the average consumer. For example, emergency phone calls are made possible by compact power sources, such as nickel-metal hydride and lithium-ion batteries (No. 15). Without them, cellphones would be far less dependable and not rechargeable. Also, flash memory (No. 22) has made the digital camera (No. 9) possible and has changed the way people transport data.

Some of the inventions on the list have brought to life science-fiction concepts. Among them are the space shuttle (No. 20), which advanced space exploration, and hybrid cars (No. 16), which pollute less. Interestingly, the innovation that laid the groundwork for many of the inventions mentioned above is found underground, where fibre optics (No. 4) has helped turn the world into a global village.

Illustration

eBook Extra

Responding

What Do You Think Now? What is the most important technological innovation in your life? Did your choice change after reading this article? Explain.

Determining Main Ideas: What is the main idea of this article? What helped you determine the main idea?

Summarizing: Magazine editors often include a summary at the start of an article. Write a brief introductory summary for this article.

Reading Like a Writer: Explain why the journalist used numbers in parentheses throughout the article. What else could have been done to achieve the same goal?

Evaluating: Of the top 25 innovations in this text, which ones have the greatest impact on your life? Why? Would your parents choose the same innovations? Explain.

Metacognition: How did you organize your ideas for your summary? Did you include only important information? Did you express a personal opinion? Explain.

What do you think?

Human innovations often create more harm than good.

Strongly Disagree				Strongly Agree
1	2	3	4	5

FRANKENSTEIN

Graphic Fiction by Scott Hepburn and colourist Espen Grundetjern
Based on the Novel by Mary Wollstonecraft Shelley

VICTOR REALIZES HIS CREATION IS GROTESQUE, A MONSTER THAT IS MORE ANIMAL THAN HUMAN. HE FLEES IN FEAR.

What have I done?

ALONE AND ENRAGED, THE MONSTER TAKES REVENGE ON ITS CREATOR BY KILLING VICTOR'S BROTHER.

VICTOR LEARNS THE CONSEQUENCES OF TRYING TO CREATE LIFE.

My brother, I'm so sorry.

HUMANS AND ANIMALS ALIKE ARE TERRIFIED OF THE MONSTER!

THE MONSTER MUST DISCOVER THE WORLD ALONE.

I'll return shortly, grandfather.

THE MONSTER LEARNS AN IMPORTANT LESSON: FIRE CAN LIGHT THE WAY, BUT CAN ALSO CAUSE GREAT PAIN. AND ANOTHER HUMAN DIES AS THE SIMPLE COTTAGE BURNS.

THE MONSTER SEARCHES FOR HAPPINESS.

MEANWHILE, VICTOR SEEKS SOLITUDE. THE MONSTER FINDS HIM AND GREETS ITS CREATOR WITH PURPOSE, INSTEAD OF RAGE.

YOU GAVE ME LIFE, BUT YOU DENIED ME LOVE. I SHALL REMAIN ALONE UNLESS YOU HELP ME. I BEG YOU TO CREATE A MATE FOR ME.

VICTOR FEELS COMPELLED TO CREATE A MATE.

This is the least I can do to correct my mistake.

ULTIMATELY, HOWEVER, VICTOR CAN'T BEAR TO CREATE ANOTHER MONSTER. HE THROWS IT INTO THE SEA.

My creations are not progress.

YOU'RE THE MONSTER!

VICTOR IGNORES THE MONSTER AND RETURNS HOME.

AGAIN, THE MONSTER TAKES ITS REVENGE, KILLING VICTOR'S NEW WIFE.

VICTOR SETS OFF ON A QUEST TO KILL THE MONSTER, BUT DIES BEFORE HE CAN.

THE MONSTER IS CHASED INTO THE ICY MOUNTAINS ...

DESTINED TO DIE ALONE.

eBook Extra

Responding

What Do You Think Now? Do human innovations often create more harm than good? Do selfish intentions sometimes influence what we do with innovations or the direction of our technological advances? Explain.

Determining Main Ideas: What is the main idea of this graphic text? What helped you determine it?

Summarizing: Summarize this graphic text in five sentences. Be sure to express its supporting details in clear and concise language.

Evaluating Graphic Text: Have the artists effectively used both graphic and print features? What helped you most to understand the text: the graphics or the written text? Explain.

Reading Like a Writer: Describe the voice of the text and the impression it leaves on the reader. Why do you think this voice was used?

Critical Thinking: Is this graphic text a warning to humankind to evaluate the motivation behind innovation or is it a comment about society and humanity? Explain.

Metacognition: Describe the strategies or process you used to help you determine the main idea and summarize this graphic text. How effectively did the strategies or process work for you?

APPLYING READING STRATEGIES

▶ Determining Main Ideas
▶ Summarizing

VOCABULARY

paramount: of chief concern or importance

Vocabulary Tip

If you encounter a new word, it often helps to read further in the passage. For example, the meaning of the word *paramount* is not clear in the sentence "Speed is paramount." However, the rest of the paragraph stresses the importance of being first with a news story, so you can guess that *paramount* means "important."

What do you think?

The accuracy of information received is more important than the speed with which it is received.

Strongly Disagree				Strongly Agree
1	2	3	4	5

JEREMY GUTSCHE
MISTER CHAOS

Newspaper Feature by Cathal Kelly

Jeremy Gutsche is explaining how I should write my Jeremy Gutsche article.

"Now, you're going to do one article, an in-depth piece," says Jeremy. He is disappointed.

"The majority of your traffic comes from search engines. So one article, well, that's no good. You need to break the story into a Jeremy Gutsche interview, an *Exploiting Chaos* [Jeremy's new book] interview, a Trendhunter [Jeremy's website] interview, and maybe a couple of other things. In a newspaper, it'd look ridiculous. Online, you've created four or five options for the search engines to find. That's the future, in a nutshell."

Jeremy is the founder of the Trendhunter website, a constantly changing site dedicated to identifying the latest big thing. And by "latest" we mean, like, 15 minutes ago.

While running a billion-dollar credit card company, Jeremy began building Trendhunter at night. He taught himself how to code and design. He hung in for "one last bonus" before heading out on his own three years ago.

Jeremy initially saw Trendhunter as a virtual community to discuss business ideas. He eventually realized the website *was* the idea. Today, 28 000 global "trend hunters" contribute ideas—from baby Jacuzzis to pet piercings. They are sifted by the Trendhunter staff, repackaged, resifted, and posted—100 of them every day. Recent contributions include 99 Bizarre Toys and TV-Themed High Tops.

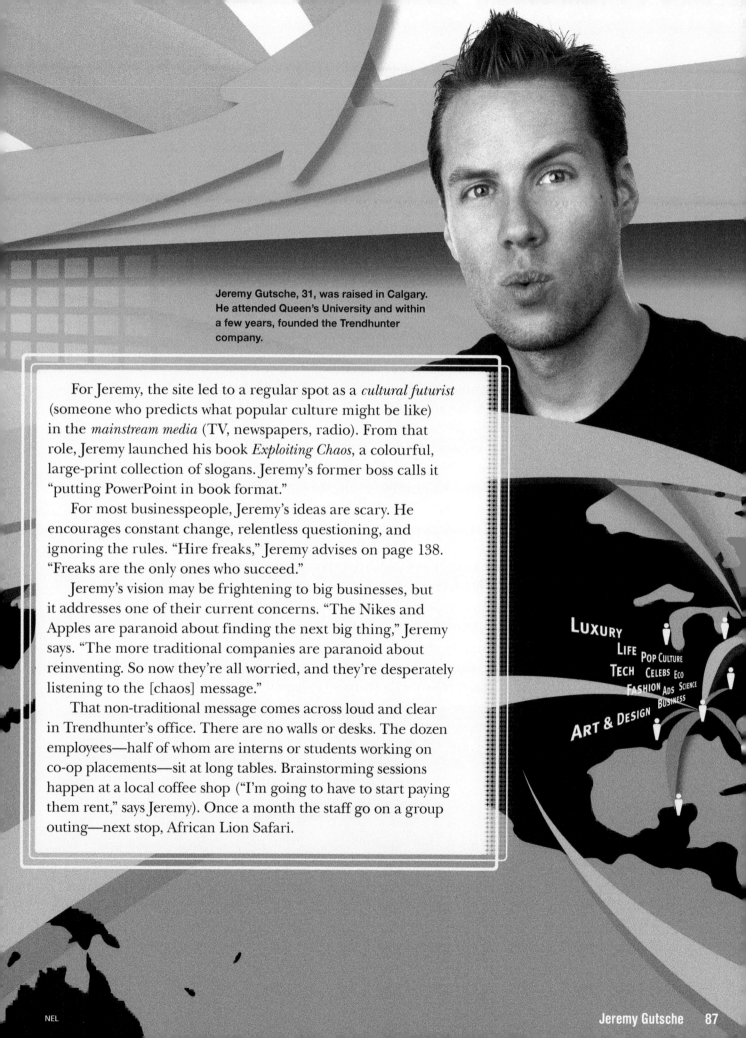

Jeremy Gutsche, 31, was raised in Calgary. He attended Queen's University and within a few years, founded the Trendhunter company.

For Jeremy, the site led to a regular spot as a *cultural futurist* (someone who predicts what popular culture might be like) in the *mainstream media* (TV, newspapers, radio). From that role, Jeremy launched his book *Exploiting Chaos*, a colourful, large-print collection of slogans. Jeremy's former boss calls it "putting PowerPoint in book format."

For most businesspeople, Jeremy's ideas are scary. He encourages constant change, relentless questioning, and ignoring the rules. "Hire freaks," Jeremy advises on page 138. "Freaks are the only ones who succeed."

Jeremy's vision may be frightening to big businesses, but it addresses one of their current concerns. "The Nikes and Apples are paranoid about finding the next big thing," Jeremy says. "The more traditional companies are paranoid about reinventing. So now they're all worried, and they're desperately listening to the [chaos] message."

That non-traditional message comes across loud and clear in Trendhunter's office. There are no walls or desks. The dozen employees—half of whom are interns or students working on co-op placements—sit at long tables. Brainstorming sessions happen at a local coffee shop ("I'm going to have to start paying them rent," says Jeremy). Once a month the staff go on a group outing—next stop, African Lion Safari.

LUXURY

LIFE POP CULTURE

TECH CELEBS ECO

FASHION ADS SCIENCE

BUSINESS

ART & DESIGN

Jeremy's company operates as a testing ground for the creative workplace he advocates. The creative chaos extends beyond the office onto the web. Trendhunter undergoes nearly constant tweaking. An entire site redesign is often done in a day. At a major corporation or a mainstream news site, that process takes months.

Speed is paramount. Trendhunter's senior editor, Bianca Bartz, recalls the thrill of being the first to post the news that Paris was allowing the only skyscraper development in the city's history. She found the news on a German site. Yahoo quickly picked up on the story, generating off-the-chart traffic at the Trendhunter website.

"It turned out to be a hoax," Bianca says, as an afterthought. "You know, a lot of people don't trust what we do. We aren't able to fact-check everything. But other newspapers or Yahoo or whoever are publishing what we find because they don't want to miss anything."

As a content provider—still Trendhunter's core mission—it sits at the contested intersection of old and new media.

Trendhunter (and similar sites, like Daily Beasts and Gawkers) need old media for content. The old media—the established news organizations—increasingly need the new media to spread their message. Depending on your perspective, it's a negative or positive relationship.

"In the long run, this is going to be a good thing for journalists, though many of them can't appreciate it right now," says Lisa George, an economist who studies the media at New York's Hunter College.

online
cultural futurist
Gutsche

future

community
LUXURY
LIFE POP CULTURE
TECH CELEBS ECO
FASHION ADS SCIENCE
BUSINESS
ART & DESIGN

people

website

cultural futurist
study

capitalist   billion-dollar

She points out, "Newspapers may or may not exist in the future. But there will be a market for individual content providers. However, this may well be a winner-take-all market. The journalists who are not as well known, the ones who can't generate traffic—they may not have jobs."

At this point, traffic is the greatest money-maker for Trendhunter. Internet ads bring in enough money that top contributors can earn up to $2000 a month, according to Jeremy. Trendhunter also does tailored trend reports for businesses like Microsoft, Holt Renfrew, and eBay. The $1500 fee for a single one of these pays a month's rent on the office.

As for the future, that's difficult to say. Remember— relentless change. Jeremy has already started a second book on a topic yet to be named. "Right now, this feels like a hobby," he says, shrugging. "If it ever gets boring, there's an opportunity to use Trendhunter as a launching point for some new product."

It's not difficult to bask in Jeremy's relentless positivity.

"You're going to be okay," Jeremy coos to me. "You've got 188 000 search engine hits on your name."

"Really?"

"Sure. You're easy to find at this point. You're a legend!"

eBook Extra

Responding

What Do You Think Now? Is the accuracy of information received more important than the speed with which it is received? How would news networks respond to this question?

Determining Main Ideas: What is the broad topic of this article? How do the main points in the article relate to the topic? What main idea do they express?

Summarizing: Summarize the article's main idea and supporting points in five sentences.

Making Inferences: What can you infer about Jeremy? What does he value? How do you know that?

Reading Like a Writer: This writer uses jargon—phrases like *mainstream media* and *cultural futurist*. Why is jargon like that appropriate in this article? What strategies do you use to understand jargon?

Evaluating: In your opinion, is Trendhunter a reliable or unreliable compiler of news? Explain.

Media Literacy: How effectively has the designer reflected the content of this selection? What else might he or she have done?

Metacognition: What steps did you take to help you summarize this newspaper article?

How to

IDENTIFY THE ELEMENTS OF A BIOGRAPHY

Distinguishing Between Biography and Autobiography

A biography is the story of a person's life as told by someone else; an autobiography is the story of a person's life as told by him- or herself.

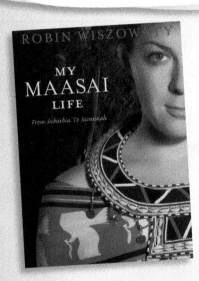

ROBIN WISZOWATY

MY MAASAI LIFE
From Suburbia To Savannah

A biography is the story of a person's life written by another person. It usually provides a description of the individual's career and life, as well as insights into his or her feelings, thoughts, and social environment. A biography may also highlight very personal experiences and provide an analysis of those experiences.

CHARACTERISTICS OF A BIOGRAPHY

- provides a description of how the person has influenced, or been influenced by, the environment in which he or she lived
- provides details to illustrate the person's accomplishments, goals, attitudes, and behaviours
- explains how the person's ideas, discoveries, or accomplishments have affected others
- includes quotations from the person, as well as quotations from others about the person
- implicitly or explicitly states how the writer feels about the person
- organized chronologically or by cause and effect; may include flashbacks to help readers understand how past events influence future events

ELEMENT OF STYLE

The level of language you use when writing a biography is determined by your subject, purpose, and audience.

	INFORMAL	FORMAL
LEVEL OF LANGUAGE	casual, everyday; some slang; contractions	often specialized; technical; no slang; no contractions
SENTENCE AND PARAGRAPH STRUCTURE	short and simple sentences; sentence fragments; short paragraphs	all sentences complete; variety of sentence types; paragraphs are fully developed
TONE	conversational, casual; sounds like ordinary speech	serious, impersonal

THE FORMAL VS. CONTEMPORARY BIOGRAPHY

Although all biographers attempt to tell the story of another person's life, how they tell the story can vary dramatically.

Formal Biography

- print format
- uses formal language
- divided into recognizable sections or chapters
- one author and one point of view
- once written, biography does not change

Common to Both

- tells the story of a person's life
- creates a portrait or impression of the person
- shows the bias of the writer or writers
- may include photos, maps, letters

Contemporary Biography

- uses online archives such as Facebook and MySpace
- may include videos
- often does not tell a chronological story
- multiple writers provide multiple points of view
- reader can take active role (participate in creating the biography)
- changes and evolves

Search

http://

Home

ibook Home Profile Friends Inbox

Jarome Iginla Rocks ✱1 Be a Fan

Wall Photos More

Career Highlights
- five-time NHL All-Star player
- Mark Messier Leadership Award in 2009
- assistant captain of Team Canada in the 2010 Olympics

I've been following Jarome Iginla since he was with the Kamloops Blazers. And now, he's the best right wing player in the NHL! Off the ice, Jarome enjoys spending time with his family and getting involved in his community. Between the years 2000 and 2005, Jarome donated $1000 for every goal he scored to KidSport Canada.

In 2005, he doubled that amount to $2000 per goal. His former manager, Craig Button, says, "[Jarome is] a better person than he is a player, and we all know what kind of player he is." And that couldn't be truer!

Abe Vusina
We put it in the win column tonight! Jarome rocked—again. Check out the photos I posted to see our guy in action.
3 minutes ago

Ellie Hamil
He should be captain for Team Canada! Everyone agree?
2 days ago

Transfer Your Learning

Connect to ...

Careers: Why might someone find it helpful to read the biographies of successful entrepreneurs?

Media: Biographies of famous people can often be found in both the form of written texts and multimedia TV programs. Which biographical form do you prefer? Why?

What do you think?

More than anywhere else, people with big ideas are needed to fight for the environment.

Strongly Disagree				Strongly Agree
1	2	3	4	5

SHEILA WATT-CLOUTIER

THE LIFE AND TIMES OF AN INUIT ACTIVIST

Biography by Carmen Jones

VOCABULARY

dire: urgent and ominous

Vocabulary Tip

Skilled writers choose adjectives carefully. In the phrase "dire consequences," the adjective *dire* creates a greater sense of urgency than if the writer had chosen *harmful* or *negative*.

HERITAGE

Sheila Watt-Cloutier was born in Kuujjuaq, an Inuit village in the region of Nunavik, in northern Québec on December 2, 1953.

Of her heritage, Sheila has said, "I am part of a generation that has experienced tumultuous change in a very short period of time. We have come from a traditional world to a high-tech way of life. In 51 years, I have come from travelling by dog team and canoe to flying jumbo jets all over the world.... Our families and communities have been shaken by the change from a strong, independent way of life—living and learning from the land with our own education, judicial, social, and economic systems—to a way of life highly dependent on substances, institutions, and processes.... However, powerless victims we are not. The Inuit culture not only survived but also thrived harmoniously with nature in what people call the harshest environment in the world. We invented homes of snow, warm enough for our babies to sleep in naked. We invented the *qajaq*, the most ingeniously engineered boat. Inuit won't disappear or be wiped out by globalization. Rather, we hope our destiny is to light a beacon for the world."

POLITICAL CAREER

Sheila has been a political spokesperson for Inuit for over a decade. From 1995 to 1998, she worked as the Corporate Secretary of the Makivik Corporation. In that position, Sheila oversaw the administration of the Inuit claim under the James Bay and Northern Québec Agreement.

Sheila was elected president of the Inuit Circumpolar Conference (ICC), Canada, in 1995, and was re-elected in 1998. The ICC defends the rights and interests of Inuit in Russia, Alaska, Canada, and Greenland. As ICC president, Sheila played an important role in the negotiation of the 2001 Stockholm Convention. This agreement banned the creation and use of persistent organic pollutants (POPs). POPs have been proven to pollute the Arctic food web. Sheila explained the impact, by saying, "Inuit are being poisoned from afar by toxins—PCBs, DDT, and other chemicals—carried to the Arctic on air currents. These chemicals contaminate the food web we depend upon, seals, whales, walruses, and end up in our bodies and the nursing milk of our mothers in high levels. So what a world we have created when Inuit women have to think twice about nursing their babies."

The strength of Sheila's voice increased when she was elected International Chair of the ICC in 2002. In that position she spoke out against climate change and fought for Inuit rights. Sheila held her position with the ICC until 2006. Since then, she has left elected politics, but remains a vocal advocate for human rights and environmental preservation.

← **Understanding Biography**

Biographers often provide insight into how the person has influenced, or been influenced by, the environment or society in which he or she lives. What insight does this passage give you about Sheila Watt-Cloutier?

The next generation, the younger generation, has to be adding a lot of pressure onto the powers that be because this is their future.

Understanding Biography →

Biographers often directly or indirectly reveal their opinions about the people they are writing about. What opinion is revealed in this biography?

Understanding Biography →

A biography provides insight into what a person values and believes is important. What does Sheila value? What does she believe is important? How do you know?

ACTIVISM

In recent years, Sheila has become an environmental and Inuit hero. She won this status by speaking out in many media interviews and in documentaries, such as *The Great Warming* (2006). She has also fought for Inuit interests in front of several Canadian government commissions and United Nations panels. As an activist, Sheila is able to "put a human face" on the devastation caused by climate change.

In December 2005, Sheila joined 62 Inuit hunters and Elders from communities across Canada and Alaska to launch one of the world's first international legal actions on climate change. The group submitted a petition to the Inter-American Commission on Human Rights (IACHR). It suggested that unchecked emissions of greenhouse gases from the United States have violated Inuit cultural and environmental human rights. The 167-page petition examined the harmful effects of global warming on Arctic geography, wildlife, human health, and culture, and outlined the dire consequences for the Inuit hunting-based society and economy.

Sheila Watt-Cloutier became an Officer of the Order of Canada in 2006.

↙ **Understanding Biography**

A biography includes quotations. What does this quotation tell you about Sheila and what she's interested in?

> ❝ **Global warming connects us all.... The Inuit hunter who falls through the depleting and unpredictable sea ice is connected to the cars we drive, the industries we rely upon, and the disposable world we have become. ❞**

On March 1, 2007, she testified before the Commission during its extraordinary first hearing on the links between climate change and human rights. She noted, "Climate change threatens our very survival as peoples."

Since her testimony at the IACHR, Sheila has travelled around the world, sharing her message in the media, at conferences, and other speaking engagements. Her activism has challenged those in power, promoted dialogue, and changed policies to the benefit of Arctic peoples and the planet we all share.

↙ **Understanding Biography**

Revealing the impact on the world of a person's accomplishments is an important feature of biographies. What has Sheila accomplished throughout her life? How have those accomplishments affected the world?

eBook Extra

Responding

What Do You Think Now? "More than anywhere else, people with big ideas are needed to fight for the environment." How do you respond now that you've read this selection? How do you think Sheila would respond?

Understanding Biography: What impression of Sheila is created by this biography? What words or phrases create this impression?

Reading for Detail: Sheila has worked hard to stop the climatic changes faced by Inuit. Why does she believe these changes are particularly threatening?

Literary Devices: "We hope our destiny is to light a beacon for the world." In this quotation, Sheila uses *symbolism* (the use of something concrete to represent something abstract). What is the symbol? What does it represent?

Critical Literacy: Which aspects of Sheila's life have been emphasized in this biography? Which aspects have been de-emphasized? Why do you think that is?

Metacognition: How did analyzing the characteristics of biographies affect your response to this biography?

VOCABULARY

culture shock: a feeling of disorientation felt by someone suddenly experiencing an unfamiliar culture or way of life

Vocabulary Tip

You can often figure out the meaning of compound words such as *culture shock* by putting together the meaning of the individual words.

What do you think?

Success in business requires innovative ideas.

Never				Always
1	2	3	4	5

TOP
OF THE
WORLD

Biographical Article by Margaret Jetelina

Bruce Poon Tip created an ecotourism company that makes over $100 million a year. He used its profits to help others around the world. Now, that's different.

Bruce Poon Tip calls himself an open book. If that's the case, then his story is a pretty good read—from his struggles as a young immigrant in Calgary to his entrepreneurial success with his global tourism company, GAP Adventures.

Bruce has journeyed the world, received numerous entrepreneurship awards, and experienced a wealth of business and personal success.

So it's easy to see why his story (which starts with his journey from Port of Spain, Trinidad, continues with his rise as a business whiz kid in Canada, and then to an international success story) is a definite page-turner. The handsome immigrant of Chinese, Dutch, and Guyanese heritage even looks the part of a multicultural hero.

How did Bruce do it? It never occurred to him that he couldn't.

After the Poon Tip family (parents and seven children) immigrated to Calgary, Bruce watched as his parents struggled to make it. His father eventually bought and managed a gas station, while his mother also worked full-time.

Coming from a relatively easy life in Trinidad, where their blended heritage was accepted in the multicultural country, the culture shock they experienced thickened the plot. "It was a real struggle when we came here. Calgary was a very tough city to [live in] in the early 1970s [for] a minority," says Bruce.

The Poon Tips were the only ethnic family in their new neighbourhood. "I often tell this story of my mother's that when she got her first job, she had arranged over the phone for daycare…. When she got there, they told her they didn't take kids of colour. She lost her job."

He and his siblings were continually treated like "others." "My brothers were always fighting to protect our sisters. We were always being chased home from school," he says. "Lucky for us, we had a big family, it was like our own little city inside our house."

Later, the family moved to a better neighbourhood, but still Bruce was only one of two visible minority students in his new school. "I remember acknowledging each other and high-fiving each other." He chuckles at the memory.

Perhaps the cultural isolation a young Bruce felt is what prompted him to start dreaming up business ideas. At 12, he started a newspaper delivery business and hired younger kids to deliver the papers.

"That was a really defining time in my life that made me what I am today," Bruce says. "There was a lack of role models, of seeing someone who can represent what you are on TV and in school. I put all that energy into my businesses where I was a leader and people listened to me."

After some post-secondary education in business and tourism, Bruce moved out to Toronto at the age of 22. "I had $800 in my pocket, and was full of stupidity, really. I thought, 'I am going to start a business and take on the world.'"

Before taking over the world, Bruce travelled around Asia to experience it. "I saw there was a gap in the travel market for people like me…. I wanted a cultural-type holiday, where I could meet local people and really experience the culture."

If Bruce is an open book, then his story is a pretty good read.

Bruce returned from his trip with the inspiration to start GAP Adventures. "When I came back, I developed my first group tour to Belize, Ecuador, and Venezuela, booking local bed and breakfasts and arranging local transportation. It was really grassroots."

Bruce certainly found a "gap" in the market. His aptly named adventure travel business has grown steadily, to the point where he sells his ecotourism tours in 27 countries and generates $100 million to $120 million a year.

"In my twenties and thirties, I was known as that 'wunderkind.' Now I'm an old has-been," jokes Bruce.

It's hardly time for his epilogue. With so much success achieved, Bruce now spends time giving back through his humanitarian organization, Planeterra.

"Our company is so connected with people, so as we became more successful, it was a no-brainer for me to give back to those communities we visit. It was the right thing to do," says Bruce, who sets a good example for his two children, Jada, 6, and Terra, 4, with his wife, Roula. "I'm a really big karma guy. I believe that you get what you give."

While Bruce struggled to find role models that looked like him when he started on his Canadian journey, he's now proud to serve as an inspiration to today's immigrants.

Bruce's tips for today's newcomers? "The first thing is to embrace the country that is now your home. You have to have an open mind. You have to venture out," he says.

As for business-specific advice, he says, "Know what your motivation is; why do you want to be an entrepreneur? You also have to fully understand what it's going to take; it's not an easy road…. So do what you love, be passionate about it, and don't be afraid to ask for help. Have the courage to get out there."

eBook *Extra*

Responding

What Do You Think Now? Does success in business require innovative ideas? How do you respond to this question now that you've read the article? Does this selection suggest that having a good idea means you'll make money? Explain.

Analyzing Biography: How is this biography organized? Do you consider the organization effective? Why or why not?

Making Inferences: What can you infer about Bruce's attitude toward life?

Critical Thinking: What does Bruce mean about being "a really big karma guy"? How does that statement affect your perception of him?

Reading Like a Writer: A direct quotation repeats someone's words exactly and uses quotation marks. An indirect quotation may paraphrase someone's words and doesn't use quotation marks. Why do you think the writer uses a mix of direct and indirect quotations from Bruce (rather than just direct quotations)?

Critical Literacy: How might some readers respond to the terms *minority* and *kids of colour*? Why has the writer included information about the racism Bruce faced?

Metacognition: How did knowing this text is a biography help you to read it?

VOCABULARY

antioxidant: a substance that inhibits the destructive effects of oxidation

enzyme: a protein produced by living cells that functions as a catalyst in biochemical reactions

gene expression: the process by which information that is coded in a gene is converted into the structures in a cell

lipid polymer combo: a biological compound (made up of identical molecules) that is not soluble in water

pharmaceuticals: the manufacture, preparation, or sale of drugs used in medicine

Vocabulary Tip

Pay attention to clues that suggest that understanding a word or phrase completely may not be essential to comprehending the larger text. Before the journalist uses the expression *lipid polymer combo*, she says, "Get this," and afterwards says, "Yeah, I know." These phrases suggest that the exact meaning of that long, technical phrase is not important to understanding the rest of the article.

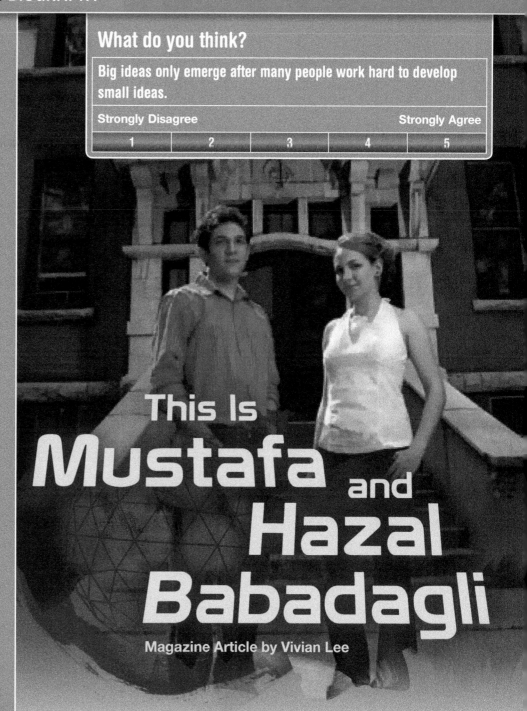

What do you think?

Big ideas only emerge after many people work hard to develop small ideas.

Strongly Disagree				Strongly Agree
1	2	3	4	5

This Is Mustafa and Hazal Babadagli

Magazine Article by Vivian Lee

"Man, you're so smart. You're going to find the cure for cancer someday."

It's a strange sort of compliment—that a high level of intellect immediately turns you into a gladiator in the battle against one of the worst diseases. Strange, but it's also heard often enough in parting yearbook messages—"Dude, go out and cure cancer! You're brill!"

The thing is, the key to this disease probably won't be found by one person. The amount of research in this field is the product of thousands of researchers, including two brilliant but still very much teenager-like 17-year-olds from Edmonton, Alberta.

Meet Mustafa and Hazal Babadagli, two teens who constantly defy the odds. This one-of-a-kind fraternal twin pair is the real deal. Last year, when they weren't cheering on soccer teams from Turkey or bonding over the TV show *What Not to Wear*, they were constructing—get this—"a non-viral vector, synthesized from a lipid polymer combo in the hopes of using SiRNA to silence the gene expression of an MMP-2 enzyme." Yeah, I know.

Today, they are taking turns explaining cancer cell migration. They describe it as calmly and as easily as if they were detailing the weather.

On the advice of their Grade 11 biology teacher, Cheryl Kachman, the twins entered the

The problem was that there are actually tons of MMP enzymes. Although the dynamic duo reduced MMP-2 levels, they didn't reduce cancer cell migration. But their work is significant. "We've created weapons that can target things in cancer cells," Mustafa says. "And results, positive or negative, are results, right?"

One result was that the pair dominated the regionals again, and flew to Ottawa to present their work to a panel of 20 judges knowledgeable in cancer research and pharmaceuticals. The judges were thoroughly impressed.

"We have a lot of family who are in the science field and we are influenced by their work," Hazal says. "Also, our mom's a pharmacist, our dad's an

> ❝This year, we wanted to do something a bit more sophisticated, something other people hadn't really done before...❞

Sanofi-Aventis BioTalent Challenge. The competition promotes high school students' interest in the field of biotechnology.

Mustafa and Hazal investigated antioxidant levels in plants. Their use of bay leaves reduced cancer cell counts by 50 percent. Because of that achievement, the twins scored first place at the regional competition and ninth at the national competition.

"This year, we wanted to do something a bit more sophisticated, something other people hadn't really done before," Mustafa explains.

What did they do? They tried to stop the production of the MMP-2 enzyme. This enzyme allows cancer cells to move around (imagine that MMP-2 is a battering ram). The idea is that if you stop cancer cells from moving around, you stop them from spreading and growing.

engineer, and with their support, along with the support of our granddad, who was a lawyer and judge, and our grandmother, who was a teacher, we have grown."

"Since our childhood, our parents have been subscribing to scientific magazines and so we've read them and our interest grows," adds Mustafa.

"I feel science is really important, and I realize that 20 to 30 years ago women weren't as dominant in this field. I think that if more women enter science competitions and contribute, it'll raise awareness and presence," Hazal says. "Science is more creative than engineering. I want to go into pharmacy and maybe do a business degree on top of that. I like learning about different drugs and how they affect the body."

"I wanted to go into engineering because I saw it as a source of innovation," says Mustafa. "When we went into the biotech challenge, I saw this whole new world of opportunity, all available through engineering. I hope to combine it with maybe bio or med school. The brain also fascinates me: diseases such as Alzheimer's or Parkinson's and how they work."

Although these two extremely ambitious individuals admit to a little friendly competition, there's a sense that they're not just siblings or lab partners, but really good friends.

"My brother is energetic, really cheerful, and practical. Sometimes he makes jokes that aren't very funny, and I tell him that but he doesn't understand," Hazal says, and concedes, "but he's a good brother."

"And Hazal is calmer than me, and hard-working," Mustafa says. "But one thing I don't like about her is she is very slow." He wants to get a reaction.

"He's trying to say I'm patient!" Hazal laughs.

"No, I mean she's slow. She makes me late for school."

It's hard to wrap one's head around all the school work, lab work, and life work these two have juggled. It's a wonder they even get seven hours of sleep each night. "Well, I had to finish a social essay on the way to Ottawa on the plane," Mustafa admits.

And the pair is definitely about more than just their biotechnology competence. Hazal loves reading historical fiction and hanging with friends. Mustafa plays classical guitar. Both like eating mac 'n' cheese.

So they are just a couple of 17-year-olds, really. But, man, if I were to write in their yearbook, it'd say this: "Mustafa and Hazal Babadagli: Go out and cure cancer or Parkinson's or Alzheimer's someday. Go out and change the world with the brains and heart and passion you both possess. Because if anyone can do it, it's you guys. You're brill."

eBook Extra

Responding

What Do You Think Now? "Big ideas only emerge after many people work hard to develop small ideas." Why might this statement be true only in certain fields or disciplines?

Analyzing Biography: What characteristics of a biography does this selection use?

Retelling: In your own words, retell how Mustafa and Hazal's upbringing and family influenced their lives.

Critical Literacy: If this biography was turned into an autobiography, how do you think it would change?

Critical Thinking: What details make Hazal and Mustafa seem like "average" kids? Why might this be important?

Reading Like a Writer: The author doesn't really expect the reader to understand the following passage: "… a non-viral vector, synthesized from a lipid polymer combo in the hopes of using SiRNA to silence the gene expression of an MMP-2 enzyme." So why is the passage used?

Metacognition: What other text features might the author have included to help you understand the text?

What do you think?

Only innovators create music that makes a difference.

Strongly Disagree				Strongly Agree
1	2	3	4	5

EVOLUTION OF AN INSPIRATIONAL SINGER

VOCABULARY

campaigning: engaging in actions to convince others that a specific political party is worth supporting

paradigm: a pattern followed or a way of viewing the world

paradox: an apparent contradiction

Vocabulary Tip

Song lyrics, as in other forms of poetry, often require several readings before the meaning becomes clear. In this song, think about the *paradigms* (patterns) and *paradoxes* (apparent contradictions) that are described.

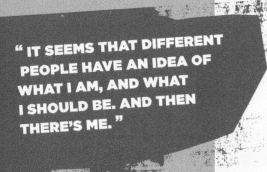

" IT SEEMS THAT DIFFERENT PEOPLE HAVE AN IDEA OF WHAT I AM, AND WHAT I SHOULD BE. AND THEN THERE'S ME. "

Biography by Laurie Thomas
Lyrics by Ani DiFranco

Ani DiFranco (born Angela Marie DiFranco on September 23, 1970) is an American musician and feminist icon. Her roots lie in Buffalo, New York, where she was raised with her older brother, Ross. Her mother, Elizabeth, grew up in Montréal and met Ani's father, Dante, when they both attended university at MIT, Boston, Massachusetts.

Growing up in Buffalo, Ani says, "I would leave the house in the morning, and I was supposed to come home when the streetlights came on, but even that was a bit stifling." Ani stayed out to avoid the chaos inside her home. She spent some of her time at guitar lessons. Her teacher recalls meeting "a little girl with pigtails down to her knees, and braces. Big smile, open eyes, a lot of wonder."

According to Ani, life at home was a "mess" until her parents separated when she was 11 years old. At that time, Ani was already singing and playing guitar in local clubs. Ani's mother was supportive of her daughter's choices and trusted her judgment.

When she was 15, Ani's parents divorced and her mother moved to Connecticut. The ever-independent Ani chose to stay in Buffalo and live with friends. She graduated from high school a year later, and spent the next few years writing and performing. By the age of 19, she had written more than 100 songs, many of them autobiographical.

PARADIGM
(from the album *Knuckle Down*, 2005)

I was born to two immigrants
Who knew why they were here
They were happy to pay taxes
For the schools and roads
Happy to be here
They took it seriously
The second job of citizenry
My mother went campaigning door to door
And holding to her hand was me

I was just a girl in a room full of women
Licking stamps and laughing
I remember the feeling of community brewing
Of democracy happening

But I suppose like anybody
I had to teach myself to see
All that stuff that got lost
On its way to church
All that stuff that got lost
On its way to school

All that stuff that got lost
On its way to the house of my family
All that stuff that was not lost on me

Teach myself to see each of us
Through the lens of forgiveness
Like we're stuck with each other (God forbid!)
Teach myself to smile and stop and talk
To a whole other color kid
Teach myself to be new in an instant
Like the truth is accessible at any time
Teach myself it's never really one or the other
There's a paradox in every paradigm

I was just a girl in a room full of women
Licking stamps and laughing
I remember the feeling of community brewing
Of democracy happening

" I HAVE SOMETHING TO PROVE,
AS LONG AS I KNOW THERE'S
SOMETHING THAT NEEDS
IMPROVEMENT, AND YOU KNOW
THAT EVERY TIME I MOVE,
I MAKE A WOMAN'S MOVEMENT. "

" I WAS BLESSED WITH A BIRTH AND A DEATH, AND I GUESS I JUST WANT SOME SAY IN BETWEEN. "

Ani took these songs with her when she moved to New York City in 1989. There she attended college classes, worked part-time jobs, and sang her heart out. In 1990, Ani created Righteous Babe Records.

Ani's popularity grew and in 1991 she toured across the United States. By 1993, she was regularly approached by major labels—and regularly rejected their offers. She didn't need them; her own label was doing well. What began as a "joke" became a thriving business and a political statement: this artist would not be owned.

" WE HAVE TO BE ABLE TO CRITICIZE WHAT WE LOVE, TO SAY WHAT WE HAVE TO SAY, 'CAUSE IF YOU'RE NOT TRYING TO MAKE SOMETHING BETTER, THEN AS FAR AS I CAN TELL, YOU ARE JUST IN THE WAY. "

In 1994, the media latched onto Ani. So did her fans, who identified with her autobiographical and political music and enjoyed her intensely personal shows.

Ani's musical success continued. In 2004 she won a Grammy Award for Best Recording Package for her record *Evolve*. Two years later, Ani received the "Woman of Courage Award" at the National Organization for Women Conference and Youth Summit. This award recognized how Ani has fought for human rights and supported various grassroots cultural and political organizations.

Although she continues to make music, Ani's focus has shifted slightly. In 2007, Ani gave birth to Petah Lucia DiFranco Napolitano. Ani's twentieth record, *Red Letter Year*, deals mainly with love and motherhood, but she remains committed to political causes. Her website hosts an "ACTION" forum that allows fans to share ideas and stories about positive social change.

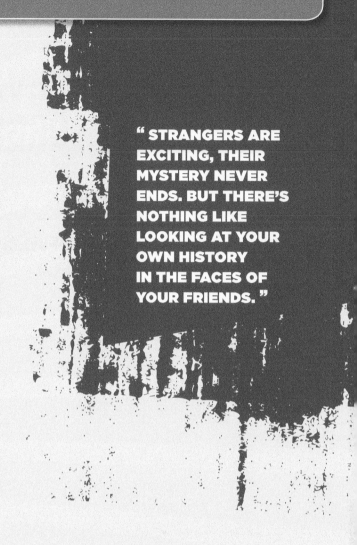

" STRANGERS ARE EXCITING, THEIR MYSTERY NEVER ENDS. BUT THERE'S NOTHING LIKE LOOKING AT YOUR OWN HISTORY IN THE FACES OF YOUR FRIENDS. "

eBook*Extra*

Responding

What Do You Think Now? "Only innovators create music that makes a difference." How do you respond now that you've read this selection? How might Ani DiFranco respond?

Analyzing Biography: How might this biography differ if it was in the form of a contemporary biography, such as a Facebook profile? What different insights might the reader gain about Ani DiFranco's life?

Literary Devices: Reread the song, thinking about how Ani uses repetition. What effect does the repetition of certain lines and words have on the listener?

Critical Literacy: Imagine that a brief paragraph, written from the perspective of a major recording-label executive, were added to this biography. What might it say? Would it be likely to commend or criticize Ani as a musician? Explain.

Evaluating: Compare the lyrics from Ani's autobiographical song "Paradigm," to her biography. How are the stories similar? How are they different?

Metacognition: In what ways has your understanding of how to create a biography been improved by reading biographies?

How to

DEVELOP AND ORGANIZE IDEAS

The writing process begins when you develop ideas and decide how you will organize those ideas. These steps are often neglected, but they are critical to good writing.

DEVELOPING IDEAS

Ideas are the "what" of your writing—they are what you have to say about your topic. Your ideas will be clear, focused, and easy to understand if you know exactly what you are writing about, why you are writing, and who you are writing for.

Recipe for Developing Ideas

1. Understand your topic, purpose, and audience.

2. Upon completing your research, narrow your topic to one idea.

3. Develop your main idea with supporting details (use a graphic organizer to help you organize your writing).

4. Always start writing with a full tank of gas—enough knowledge about your topic.

TOPIC	AUDIENCE AND PURPOSE
• Research your topic to explore related ideas and improve your focus.	• Always write with a specific purpose and audience in mind.
• Determine what you know and what you don't know. Then fill in the gaps.	• Select the best organizational pattern and form for your audience and purpose.
• Separate important information from unimportant information.	• Anticipate your audience's needs.
• Connect supporting details to expand your ideas.	• Decide which ideas and supporting details best reflect your purpose.

I want to create a graphic comic that retells Louis Riel's story.

I know a great website with loads of information on him.

ORGANIZING IDEAS

Often your purpose will determine the form you choose and the way you organize your writing. The following chart shows some examples.

PURPOSE	POSSIBLE FORMS	POSSIBLE TEXT PATTERNS
to inform or explain	• report • *business letter* • e-mail • paragraph • essay	cause-and-effect, compare-and-contrast, question-and-answer, problem-solution, recount, *sequence*
to narrate or tell a story	• biography • short story • personal letter • song	narrative, recount, *sequence*
to entertain	• script • comic • poetry • *picture book* • song	narrative, recount, *sequence*, sonnet, limerick, haiku, *ballad*
to persuade	• paragraph • essay • review • editorial • song	generalization, compare-and-contrast, problem-solution

Using a graphic can help you organize your ideas as you start writing. Here are some good graphic organizers for some common text patterns.

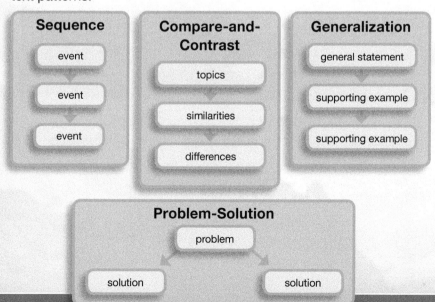

Sequence
event → event → event

Compare-and-Contrast
topics
similarities
differences

Generalization
general statement
supporting example
supporting example

Problem-Solution
problem
solution — solution

Transfer Your Learning

Connect to ...

Technology: How do you use technology to help you develop or organize ideas?

Oral Communication: If you were interviewing someone as part of your research for a writing assignment, how would good listening and speaking help you develop your ideas?

UNDERSTANDING
WRITING
STRATEGIES

Reading Like a Writer

▶ Developing and
Organizing Ideas

VOCABULARY

bantered: teased with humour

inception: the beginning

medium: the means by which something is communicated

muses: says something thoughtfully

Vocabulary Tip

The plural form of the word *medium* (meaning "the means by which something is communicated) is *media*. The plural noun requires a plural verb ("Several media *were* used to create the exhibit").

What do you think?

Communities are vital to the success of innovative business ideas.				
Never				Always
1	2	3	4	5

Jake Nickell is the CEO of Threadless.

Design That Fits to a Tee

Online Article by Laura House

Developing and Organizing Ideas

Writers need to establish the topic of their writing early in the text. What is the topic in this article? How do the ideas in the article support the topic?

➡ What began as a design submission for an online contest has spooled into the thriving T-shirt business and web-based community Threadless. Now a multi-million dollar enterprise selling more than 90 000 tees a month, this is the little community-based design company that could.

time T addition

addition

These T-shirt designs are the work of independent designers.

Central to its success are its independent designers and supporting community. Here's how it works: the site holds ongoing open calls for T-shirt designs, which are then scored and critiqued by over 650 000 registered users; next, the winning designs are printed and sold. This medium offers wide exposure for budding designers, and an affordable way for people to support independent artists. And of course there's the benefit of having something unique to wear, cooler than the average mall gear.

Jake Nickell, a self-described "entrepreneurial madman," is the founder and CEO of Threadless. In 2000, while a student at the Illinois Institute of Art in Chicago, Jake entered a design contest on the now-defunct Dreamless website. The challenge was to create the official T-shirt for an event in London. Jake's design won the competition—a perk for an art student. However, the greater reward was the exposure to a unique online community of designers.

The Dreamless website "was a great environment for hobbyists and professionals alike to unleash creativity," Jake says. Artists chatted online, shared critiques, and bantered in mock design battles. It was through this online forum that Jake met his first partner, Jacob DeHart. Although no longer with Threadless, Jacob was crucial to its inception.

Inspired by the London contest, Jake and Jacob decided to host another design competition. They posted it as a thread on the Dreamless forum with the apt title "Threadless."

"We thought it would be a fun project that would give back to the community by actually making goods out of the work created by these artists," Jake explains. "We started it as a hobby … just a way to enhance the Dreamless community."

The winning design was then printed on T-shirts and sold. Any profits were put toward hosting another competition and printing more winning designs. For the first few rounds, winning designers received a few free tees, but by 2002 Threadless was able to award a $100 cash prize.

Developing and Organizing Ideas

Thoughtful writers have a specific audience and purpose in mind as they write. Who do you think is the target audience of this article? What do you think is its purpose?

Anyone can be a designer. Even kids design T-shirts for Threadless.

Jake and Jacob each invested $500 to fund these competitions, which they began hosting on the Threadless site. As Threadless expanded, they created the umbrella company skinnyCorp to launch other online projects and communities. "For those first two years, every dime we earned from selling tees just went right back into printing more of them," recalls Jake. Not only were funds tight, but their free time was, too. Jake and Jacob each worked full-time jobs, while attending college and running the business on the side.

By 2003 it was clear that this was more than just a hobby. Jake and Jacob scouted office space, quit their jobs, and even hired their first employee. Although not profitable yet, Threadless proved that they could build an e-commerce website.

By 2004 they had outgrown their roughly 275-square-metre space. Two years later they were up to 18 employees and running the operation from their current 7620-square-metre facility. The team took on an investor, Insight Venture Partners, to manage the rapid growth. Jake admits, "I'm much more interested in the creative, fun side of the business. It's nice to have someone with expertise who is invested in the business to help us figure out all the boring stuff."

It seems like a simple concept, this T-shirt business, but visit the site to catch a glimpse of why this model has thrived. It doesn't float adrift in cyberspace. Threadless has sparked a vibrant, involved community with an inviting, friendly vibe. Members can check in on designers, keep up with celebrity tee sightings, rate submissions, or chat with other like-minded members. When asked if he ever dreamed the community would expand as it has, Jake says, "I did not envision it to be as large as it is. I think that having a variety in the designs that get chosen is pretty important in keeping the community fresh. To be able to see design trends come and go is important, and we always need to be on top of what is cool at any given moment."

Threadless has a flagship retail and gallery space in Chicago.

Today, winners receive a sizable cash prize ($2000), get extra exposure with an interview slot on the site and, more importantly, they get to see their designs everywhere.

The designer success stories are impressive, too. "Tokidoki is a great example of an artist who has gained huge exposure since being printed on Threadless," Jake points out. He is referring to the Italian artist Simone Legno, who has gone on to collaborate with other manufacturers of commercial goods. Another success story is Glenn Jones, who "recently started up his own T-shirt site and left his full-time job due to his fame and success on Threadless."

Proving that commercial success need not be dull, the Threadless empire continues to evolve. In fall 2007, its first retail space, or community centre, opened in Chicago. There is a store at street-level and an interactive space upstairs used for gallery shows promoting independent artists, design classes, and other special events. The company has also created its own private label to further perfect the end product. As for the future, Jake muses, "We plan to continue to grow the awesomeness levels to new, previously unreached heights." And as with all things Threadless, we users will be the judge.

Developing and Organizing Ideas

Writers use text patterns that best suit the topic, purpose, and audience of their texts. As you read the article, what pattern did you identify? Does this pattern make sense given the topic, purpose, and audience? Explain.

eBook *Extra*

Responding

What Do You Think Now? Are communities vital to the success of innovative business ideas? Would the owner of Threadless agree with this statement? Would other entrepreneurs also agree? Explain.

Reading Like a Writer: If you were to insert headings into the text to support its organization, where would you insert them? Write an appropriate heading for each section you identified.

Reading for Detail: Identify and explain the main reasons for the success of Threadless.

Making Inferences: What sacrifices has Jake Nickell made to help his innovative business succeed? What can you infer about his character and business sense?

Evaluating: Does the last line effectively bring the article to an end? Why or why not?

Media Literacy: If you were to enter a Threadless T-shirt contest, what would your T-shirt design look like? What would you most want to get out of entering the contest?

Literary Devices: The author uses an allusion by referring to the "little company that could" (making the reader think of "the little engine that could"). How does this allusion affect your view of Threadless? What tone does it set for the selection?

Metacognition: Do you find developing ideas for your writing challenging? What strategies do you use to help you develop ideas?

APPLYING
WRITING
STRATEGIES

Reading Like a Writer

▶ Developing and
Organizing Ideas

WORLDWIDE WE

Article by Cheryl Gilbert

The Free The Children movement is a formidable force. At its core are groups of idealistic youth.

Every social movement starts somewhere. This movement started with Craig Kielburger, a small group of Grade 7 students, and their initiative to stop child poverty and exploitation: Free The Children. Through empowerment programs and leadership training, Free The Children inspires more than one million young people to be socially conscious global citizens.

Today, the organization has two goals. The first is to free children from poverty by providing them with schools, clean water, health care, alternative sources of income, and other resources they need to live healthier lives.

The second goal is to free young people from the idea that they are powerless to affect positive change in the world. Often, people believe that only adults can make a difference. Craig and the team at Free The Children know this isn't true.

VOCABULARY

empowerment: to give power or authority

formidable: inspiring respect or wonder because of size, strength, or ability

idealism: the promotion or pursuit of noble principles, purposes, or goals

initiative: a plan or task that is energetically pursued

Vocabulary Tip

Words often have connotations, or added meanings. For example, if a force is *formidable*, it is more than just powerful. It also inspires respect or fear.

1995

Free The Children begins. Twelve-year-old Craig and 11 of his Grade 7 classmates start a group dedicated to raising awareness about child labour.

1996

Craig holds a press conference urging Prime Minister Jean Chrétien to address child labour. The prime minister agrees to meet with Craig. Free The Children soon gains international recognition.

THE FUEL

According to Craig, the success of Free The Children is due to the idealism of youth. "People called us idealistic," Craig says of Free The Children in its early days. "We still are. In fact, we're shamelessly idealistic." That idealism was infectious. It spread from Craig's small group to thousands of supporters in 45 countries. They all shared the same belief: their small actions would collectively change lives.

Eventually, they looked to the idealistic Me to We philosophy for inspiration. The philosophy is based on the belief that each choice a person makes doesn't just affect "me," it affects "we"—the world around us. Thanks to this philosophy, Craig's small spark spread into a fiery global initiative.

Craig meets the Dalai Lama.

WHAT "WE" HAS ACCOMPLISHED

To date, Free The Children has

- built over 500 schools

- provided education to over 50 000 children

- distributed over 207 000 school and health kits

- shipped over $15 million worth of medical supplies

- built health care centres for over 512 000 people

- equipped more than 23 500 women to be economically self-sufficient

- improved access to clean water, health care, and sanitation for over 650 000 people

1999

Craig appears on Oprah to discuss his work with Free The Children. As a result, millions of people are inspired by Craig's fight to end child labour.

2002

Free The Children is nominated for the Nobel Peace Prize.

2006

Free The Children wins the World's Children's Prize for the Rights of the Child, also known as the Children's Nobel Prize. It recognizes Free The Children's outstanding contributions to the defence of children's rights.

2008

A partnership, called "O Ambassadors," is launched between Free The Children and Oprah's Angel Network. Their goal is to get 1 million North American students to take action.

2009 WE DAY CHALLENGE

- 10 actions
- 100 000 lives overseas
- 1 000 000 volunteer hours

This 2009 We Day poster outlines the goals of the movement.

FAN THE FLAMES

We Day is a series of annual events that celebrates the power of young people to change the lives of others and inspires youth to change the world. In 2009, over 32 000 students attended We Day in Vancouver and Toronto, and millions more watched televised broadcasts.

Since it began, the intention of We Day has been to inspire and engage youth to take action for change. Events feature motivational speeches by social activists, famous leaders, actors, and singers. Speakers have included an impressive number of high-profile activists, politicians, authors, singers, sports figures, and actors, such as writer and activist Robin Wiszowaty, humanitarian and motivational speaker Spencer West, MTV host Jessie Cruikshank, singers The Jonas Brothers, activist Dr. Jane Goodall, author and activist Elie Wiesel, former child soldier Michel Chikwanine, singer Sarah McLachlan, and His Holiness the Dalai Lama.

Every person who attends We Day commits to take steps for a better world. Attendees of the first two We Days raised over $5 million dollars for local, national, and international organizations. They also donated over 150 000 volunteer hours. As part of a network of students, facilitators, and educators, members of the Free The Children movement transfer their idealism into action and realize the power of young people to change the world.

We Day is dubbed a "rock concert for social change." This innovative concept educates and excites the youth that make this movement successful.

114   Unit 2: What's the Big Idea?   NEL

SPARKS SPREAD THE FIRE

Free The Children regularly celebrates the accomplishments of its members. Each year, the *Canadian Living* Me to We Awards are presented to six Canadians who have dedicated their lives to improving the lives of others. Award winners are nominated by Canadians.

In 2009, Matthew Warnock won a *Canadian Living* Me to We Award for starting the Hope to Others (H2O) organization with his sister, Kara. H2O promotes youth action, and educates and encourages youth to be environmentally friendly and aware of global issues. Matthew also started the Be the Change program, which involves him and his team making presentations at meetings, school assemblies, and conferences to raise awareness and funds for global issues.

Free The Children believes in its youth members and other supporters. They celebrate their victories and use them to inspire others to join the movement. Every youth can be inspired to become socially conscious, engaged, and active in the quest to improve lives around the world. It all starts with a spark.

Want to join the movement? One way is to take a 24-hour vow of silence with your friends. Like these students, you can raise funds for communities overseas and bring awareness to international children's rights.

eBook Extra

Responding

What Do You Think Now? Can the choices you make dramatically change the world? How might someone from Free The Children answer this question? Would you agree with them? Support your answer.

Reading Like a Writer: What seems to be the purpose of this text? What text pattern is used? Does it match the purpose? Explain.

Retelling: In your own words, explain the Me to We philosophy. Why is it considered a social movement?

Critical Literacy: How does this text affect the way you feel about the future and the role youth can play in shaping it? Explain.

Critical Thinking: How does success seem to be defined in the We movement? What do the people involved in this movement seem to value? How does this compare to other selections you've read?

Metacognition: How did reflecting about the organizational pattern of this text help you both recognize its purpose and improve your understanding of it?

APPLYING
WRITING
STRATEGIES

Reading Like a Writer

► Developing and
  Organizing Ideas

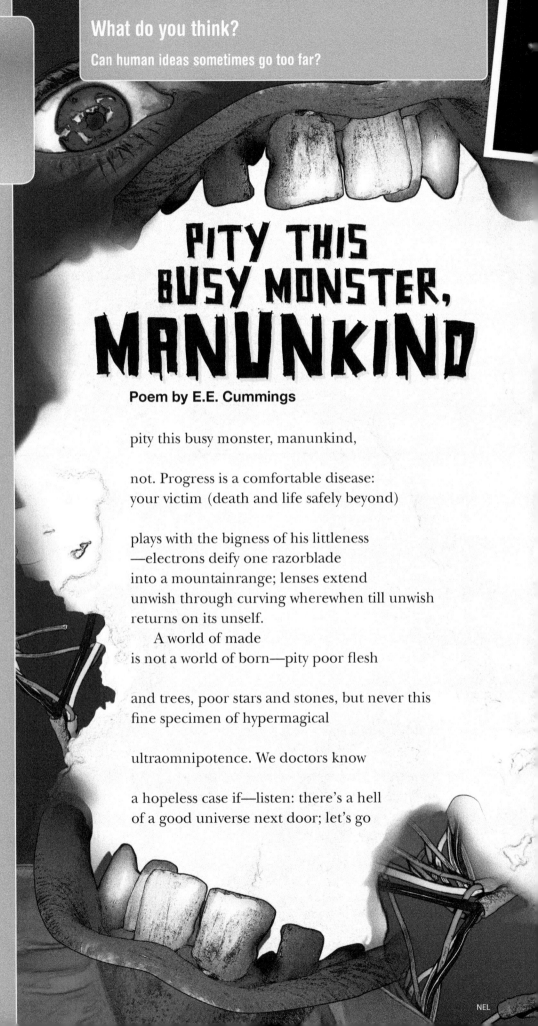

PITY THIS BUSY MONSTER, MANUNKIND

Poem by E.E. Cummings

pity this busy monster, manunkind,

not. Progress is a comfortable disease:
your victim (death and life safely beyond)

plays with the bigness of his littleness
—electrons deify one razorblade
into a mountainrange; lenses extend
unwish through curving wherewhen till unwish
returns on its unself.
        A world of made
is not a world of born—pity poor flesh

and trees, poor stars and stones, but never this
fine specimen of hypermagical

ultraomnipotence. We doctors know

a hopeless case if—listen: there's a hell
of a good universe next door; let's go

VOCABULARY

deferred: postponed

deify: to make a god of

fester: to generate pus

Vocabulary Tip

Having a rich vocabulary
brings images to life. Verbs
such as *fester*, *sag*, *crust*,
stink, and *explode* are not
normally associated with
dreams, so they create
unusual and powerful images.

Dream Deferred

Poem by Langston Hughes

What happens to a dream deferred?
Does it dry up
Like a raisin in the sun?
Or fester like a sore—
And then run?
Does it stink like rotten meat?
Or crust and sugar over—
like a syrupy sweet?
Maybe it just sags
like a heavy load.
Or does it explode?

eBook *Extra*

Responding

What Do You Think Now? "Can human ideas sometimes go too far?" How do you answer this question now that you've read these poems? How would each poet answer this question?

Reading Like a Writer: Choose one poem. Explain how the poet organized his ideas. What helped you identify the organization of this poem? Why do you think the poet chose this specific form?

Making Inferences: Choose one poem. Explain the poem's message or main idea. What is the poet's purpose and who is his audience?

Making Connections: How do both of these poems connect to the theme of this unit?

Literary Devices: In "pity this busy monster, manunkind," what does the poet compare humankind to? How appropriate is that comparison?

Evaluating: E.E. Cummings combines several words: *hypermagical, ultraomnipotence, wherewhen*. Choose one of those combined words and explain what he means.

Metacognition: Which poem did you find more difficult to understand? What made the poem difficult? Explain the strategies that helped you understand the poem.

How to

ANALYZE CODES, CONVENTIONS, AND TECHNIQUES

The people who produce media texts do so carefully and purposefully. Whether the media text is produced to entertain, persuade, or inform, the producers use a variety of codes, conventions, and techniques that they hope will appeal to their audience and send the correct message. Imagine you were hired to create an ad for a facial soap that suggested a positive connection between the soap and a healthy teen lifestyle. What images or words would you use? What images or words would you avoid using? Where would you set the ad? What music or sound effects would you use?

Producers combine the following types of codes to create effective media texts:

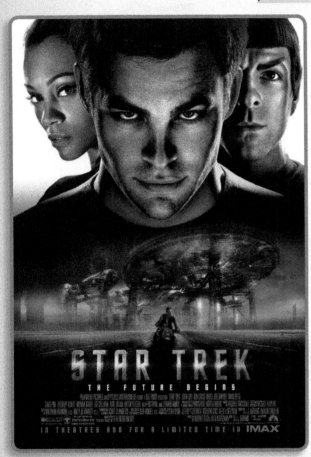

Movie posters often use similar designs. What media conventions are used in this poster? How do they compare to the conventions used in other movie posters you've seen?

- **Technical codes**—the ways producers use equipment to produce meaning—including how images are framed, camera angles, lighting, editing, and sound effects.

- **Symbolic codes**—the ways producers use nonverbal cues to produce meaning—including setting, clothing, stereotypes, position of props, body language, emotions, weather, and graphic features such as diagrams, logos, or maps.

- **Verbal and Written codes**—the ways producers use language to produce meaning—including titles, headings, speech bubbles, captions, and slogans.

COMMON MEDIA CONVENTIONS

You're more familiar with media conventions than you realize. You've been absorbing them while watching, reading, and listening to media texts since you were a baby. Visualize the scenes described in the chart on the next page and make connections to movies you've seen. For which other common scenes could you describe the conventions? Think about how producers use these conventions to "construct reality"—that is, make the scene as realistic and believable as possible.

COMMON SCENES	VIDEO CONVENTIONS
two friends arguing	• open *body language* becomes more closed and facial expressions darken as the argument begins • bright lighting • bright colours on sets and costumes • a pattern of medium shots shifts to close-ups as the argument gains intensity
someone running in fear	• dim lighting • dark colours on sets and costumes • sudden cuts between camera angles to build suspense • extreme camera angles
a young couple on a date	• bright lighting • bright colours on sets and costumes • a pattern of medium shots shifts to smiling close-ups as the couple talks • some close-ups of hand gestures and other *body language* to indicate the individuals' feelings about the date

To evaluate the effectiveness of a media text and its use of codes, conventions, and techniques, ask yourself:

1. What is the media form? Who is the text's audience and what is the text's purpose? What impact will the text have on the audience? Is that the response the media producers desired?

2. What codes do the producers use? What types of conventions and techniques are used to create meaning or construct reality?

3. What specific conventions and techniques are used? How do conventions and techniques achieve the text's purpose? Will the conventions and techniques appeal to the audience? Do they appeal to me?

4. Do the different conventions and techniques work together? If so, how? If not, why not?

5. What do the codes, conventions, and techniques tell me about what the producers value? How does that compare with what I value?

Transfer Your Learning

Connect to ...

Careers: What jobs would require you to know about codes, conventions, and techniques?

Environment: Outline the technical, symbolic, and verbal and written codes you would use in an ad for a new car that you wanted to sell to young adults concerned about the environment.

What do you think?

Sometimes a big idea for one generation provides the next generation with a brand new idea.

Strongly Disagree				Strongly Agree
1	2	3	4	5

Group of Seven Awkward Moments

Analyzing Codes, Conventions, and Techniques

Producers construct media texts with a specific purpose and audience in mind. What is the purpose and audience for this media text? As you continue reading, consider how specific codes, conventions, and techniques suggest this purpose and audience.

VOCABULARY

diorama: a three-dimensional scene, often in miniature, created by placing objects and figures in front of a painted background

human psyche: the human spirit and intellect

Vocabulary Tip

The word *psyche* has a Greek origin, meaning "mind." To figure out the meaning of the word, you might connect to similar words: *psychology, psychiatry, psychic.*

Gallery Exhibit by Diana Thorneycroft

How's this for an idea? Take a few classic Canadian paintings and brush them up with new contemporary stories. That's the brainstorm of artist Diana Thorneycroft. Her exhibit *Group of Seven Awkward Moments* was a series of photographic works or dioramas at the McMichael Gallery in Kleinberg, Ontario. Compare the original painting (below) with the image she created (opposite page) using the painting as a backdrop for her diorama.

Winter on the Don by A.J. Casson, 1926

Group of Seven Awkward Moments (Winter on the Don)
by Diana Thorneycroft, 2007

A variety of props (hockey players, puck, net, water bottle, otters) are used in this image set against the A.J. Casson painting. It shows one player (Bobby Orr) in danger and being ignored by others. The artist is suggesting that perhaps they don't see him or they see him and don't care. The guidebook says of this work, "Is their lack of response a reflection of the dark side of the human psyche—one stricken by competitiveness and jealousy wishing for their opponent's death?"

Analyzing Codes, Conventions, and Techniques

Meaning is often revealed in the ways in which "written codes" are used. What meaning is created by the title "Group of Seven Awkward Moments"?

Analyzing Codes, Conventions, and Techniques

Meaning can often be created through the careful selection and placement of images. Why have these two works of art been placed across from each other? What do you infer about the meaning they create?

● *Lake and Mountains* **by Lawren S. Harris, 1927**

Analyzing Codes, Conventions, and Techniques →

Technical codes are the ways producers use equipment to produce meaning. Think about how Diana Thorneycroft used equipment to create different effects (for example, the blurry seals and Tim Hortons sign, and the light cast on the snow in front of the hunter). What meaning is created through this usage?

Group of Seven Awkward Moments (Lake and Mountains with Double-Double) **by Diana Thorneycroft, 2008**

Of the process for using the Group of Seven paintings in her photos, Diana explains, "I either use a poster image of the original painting or I scan an image from a book which I take to a lab where I print a very large ... low-resolution reproduction of the painting. Sometimes I draw with pastel right on top of the reproduction or manipulate the image using Photoshop."

The props within Diana Thorneycroft's photographic landscapes can have many meanings. For example, the Tim Hortons sign doesn't just represent a beverage; it symbolizes our national obsession with this fast-food chain, how we connect through that cup of coffee, as well as Canadian corporate success. The white baby seals can symbolize several things to Canadians—innocence as well as the ongoing conflict between people opposed to the seal hunt and seal hunters.

Consider how the image of the hunter with a rifle is ominous, while the donuts and coffee cup add humour to the overall image. The story this image tells becomes less obvious with these additions. Who or what is the hunter pointing the gun at?

Analyzing Codes, Conventions, and Techniques

Producers of media texts carefully and strategically combine different codes, conventions, and techniques. What different codes, conventions, and techniques are used in this selection? Do they work together? Explain.

eBook Extra

Responding

What Do You Think Now? "Sometimes a big idea for one generation provides the next generation with a brand new idea." When have you revisited an idea from another generation or group? How successful was the new idea?

Analyzing Codes, Conventions, and Techniques: What codes, conventions, and techniques could have been used to make this text more effective?

Retelling: Examine one image carefully. Retell its story. Add details not found in the image. For example, what happened before and after this image was captured?

Making Judgments: If a new idea builds on an old idea, is the new idea innovative? Support your answer.

Media Literacy: Examine the image on page 121 and consider how props are used. What symbols does the artist use here? What do these symbols represent?

Critical Literacy: Who would find these dioramas amusing? Who might not? Why not?

Metacognition: How does analyzing the codes, conventions, and techniques used in this media text help you better understand its meaning?

VOCABULARY

avant-garde: daring; radical

cognitive: related to perception, memory, judgment, and reasoning

immersed: to be involved deeply in a particular activity

intuitively: based on intuition, which is the ability to understand things without the need for conscious reasoning or study

pandemics: widespread diseases

POV: point of view

Vocabulary Tip

When you encounter a new word, read what comes before it as well as what comes after it. For example, the meaning of *intuitively* is suggested by the sentence immediately before it.

0.062

Saving the World through Game Design

Blog Entry by Jane McGonigal

Jane McGonigal takes play seriously. She studies how games have an impact on the real world—and she creates mass role-playing games that do just that. Her projects include Superstruct, The Lost Ring, and World Without Oil.

Jane's games are set in near-future crisis settings, such as a world facing pandemics or mass migration. Hundreds or thousands of online players form co-operative networks and develop ingenious solutions to real challenges. Her games are amazingly realistic. For example, the recent decline of cheap gasoline in the United States produced "real" social reactions identical to the ones displayed by her games' players. Such gameplay has produced a precise forecast of social reactions. As a result, designers like Jane are moving computer games beyond entertainment; they are creating innovative ways to predict the future and explore solutions to real-world problems.

"These Games Are Experience Grenades"

FROM JANE'S ONLINE BLOG

I'm a game designer, a games researcher, and a future forecaster. I make games that care. I study how games change lives. I spend a lot of my time figuring out how the games we play today shape our real-world future. And so I'm trying to make sure that a game developer wins a Nobel Prize by the year 2032.

OK, I had a revelation. Games like Superstruct and The Lost Sport and World Without Oil and Reverse Scavenger Hunts and Tombstone Hold 'Em and SF0 missions and The Go Game are "experience grenades."

That's a new term. I thoroughly Google-checked it.

Experience grenades: You play them, and that's like pulling the pin on the grenade.

Nothing has to happen right away. Nothing has to change or be solved right away. Then, you wait. It's later—an hour later, a day later, a week later, a month later—it goes off in your head, like the delayed explosion of a grenade.

You realize: You've learned something. Your cognitive patterns are different. Your view of the possibilities in the world around you has changed. Your sense of your own potential has changed. You're ready for something you didn't even know was coming. You understand something intuitively that seems alien or confusing to others.

The thing is: This doesn't necessarily happen DURING the game. During the game, you might not believe the game is working. In the best-case scenario, you might think you're JUST having fun. Worse, the game might seem silly. You don't trust the design; it seems to be asking things of you that you don't naturally want to do. Or it might seem abstract—what's the practical takeaway? Or even worse, it might seem wonky or arbitrary or broken from your POV.

But it's working. If you're playing, the pin has been pulled. If you're really participating and immersed in the game, the work is happening in your brain. It just is. I've seen it again and again. The experience happens now, the payoff comes later.

Sometimes I know what the payoff will be; sometimes I just trust that a good game will produce something interesting. And the best thing that can happen in a game community is for players to trust that something interesting will happen, and to play as if it's an experience grenade, rather than expecting instant satisfaction.

That's a strange thing to say about a game—something we play to produce in-the-moment fun. But some games are fun later. They just are. Like the trying adventures you have that you hate at the moment but that, looking back, are the adventures of your life, the stories you cherish, the bonds you made, and the way you discovered who you could be.

Yes, that's a different kind of fun, a different kind of payoff. But games can be that, and it feels different in the moment, different than immediate and obvious fun (like Rock Band or piñatas).

I see a new class of trusted game designers who are like personal trainers. The trainer tells you to do something, and you do it—even if it HURTS! Even if it isn't fun in the moment! And the benefits come later. Not necessarily during. You trust the trainer's process and you do it to be a better person and a happier person in the long run.

There are a few designers that I trust like this: Simon Johnson, who made the Comfort of Strangers and Hip Sync; the SF0 designers; Kati London at AreaCode. If they make it, I know I can show up and play it and I will have an experience that explodes later in my mind and stays with me. I trust them and don't care what they want me to do. I know they have a design process that works and that they're trying to make people happier and more aware of the possibilities in the world around them. And I am trying to be that kind of trusted designer myself to as many people as possible.

So I thank people who show up to play my games and trust the process. People who played Superstruct—I know that experience grenade will be going off literally for months and years to come. We've already celebrated how much we've achieved during the game—but the real effects will unfold for years. That's just how they work. That's just how they're designed.

Someday I hope game designers really are seen as trusted personal trainers, and that we have the chance to take people through proven processes that pay off in the long run. More gamesight, a surprising social safety net and support system, a more engaging environment, a higher quality of life."

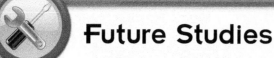

Future Studies

Jane works closely with the Institute for the Future (IFTF). The IFTF does forecasts, predicting the future. This scientific field is called Future Studies. In short, Future Studies observe major trends of where humankind is heading, near-future scenarios, and—most importantly—what kind of images and positive visions help people take sound action toward a positive future. These are complex matters, especially in times where everything is interconnected globally, yet far out of the eye, and evolving so quickly it is very difficult to keep track of them. So far, these matters have been dealt with only by a few avant-garde thinkers and high-level scientific institutions, pretty much disconnected from the rest of society that didn't understand anything ... but here comes Jane, and playfully interconnects four major fields:

- near-future scenarios
- education/learning
- positive action
- GAMING!

Gaming being THE means of bringing these fields together in a new, dynamic, participatory, inspiring experience! At last someone has done it!

eBook _Extra_

Responding

What Do You Think Now? Is creating a video game a significant innovation? If they can predict the future, who would find the information they provide useful? Explain.

Analyzing Codes, Conventions, and Techniques: What codes, conventions, and techniques common to websites or blogs did you notice in this selection? What other codes, conventions, and techniques would you use if you were designing a website or blog for Jane McGonigal?

Making Inferences: What does Jane McGonigal value in a game designer? What is she implicitly suggesting about game designers? Explain.

Summarizing: In your own words, explain what "future studies" are about. How is this field innovative?

Literary Devices: Jane uses a _metaphor_ (an implied comparison of two things) in the sentence "Games ... are 'experience grenades.'" What two things are compared? How appropriate is that comparison?

Critical Literacy: Jane believes that certain game designers and their games can lead people to "a higher quality of life." Do you agree with her? Do you think others would agree with her? Explain.

Metacognition: How did thinking about your experiences with video games help you to better understand this selection?

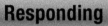

How to

USE ORAL AND VISUAL CUES TO INTERPRET TEXTS

Have you noticed that good speakers not only share information that you are interested in hearing, they also use speaking strategies that make their information appealing? These speakers have mastered the use of oral and visual cues to engage listeners and help them follow the discussion.

As a listener, it is important to recognize these cues. You will use these cues to identify key information and to interpret oral texts.

Listening Tip

Good listeners look for oral and visual cues that create emphasis or physical presence, show organization, demonstrate style, or enhance ideas. See the chart at right for more information.

CUES	EXAMPLES
Oral cues that create emphasis include statements that call a listener's attention to important information.	"Let me repeat …" "You might ask …" "You need to note …"
Oral cues that show organization include statements that help a listener understand the order, sequence, or relationship of information.	"My purpose here …" "As a result …" "So let me end …"
Oral cues that demonstrate style include the different ways that a speaker captures a listener's interest and attention.	- tone of voice, volume, and pace of speech that create emphasis - repeated words or phrases - pauses that allow the listener to absorb important information - humour used sparingly but effectively for emphasis
visual cues that create physical presence by using body language, physical movement, and facial expressions	- natural or controlled body movements to keep the listener interested or create emphasis - facial expressions to highlight important ideas or concepts
visual cues that use aids to enhance ideas	- pictures, songs, or graphics to deepen the listener's understanding - PowerPoint presentations, videos, or auditory aids to help the listener understand and interpret ideas

USE INTERPERSONAL SPEAKING SKILLS

When you speak, how you communicate your message is as important as what you say. How you **sound**, **look**, and **react** with others affects your interactions with them—positively or negatively. Developing an awareness of how you appear to others allows you to develop good interpersonal skills.

To communicate your message, and to encourage positive responses from others, ask yourself the following questions:

☑ Am I speaking at a controlled pace? Am I speaking too quickly or too loudly? Is my pace appropriate for my audience?

☑ Do my statements and responses fit with the flow of the conversation, or are they awkward and out of place?

☑ Do I vary the tone of my voice appropriately, according to the situation? Does my voice lack energy or is it too emotional?

☑ Does my posture and body language convey the desired message? Do I appear comfortable and relaxed or uneasy and nervous?

☑ Do I involve the people I am talking to by making eye contact? Do I confidently hold eye contact for a couple of seconds or do I turn away because I feel awkward?

Speaking Tip

Learn from your interactions with others. If you have had a really good conversation with someone, try to think of the reasons it went well. Remember those key points for next time. If the conversation didn't go well, try to determine what went wrong. You can learn from that experience and try again later.

Transfer Your Learning

Connect to ...

Technology: Are the interpersonal speaking skills you use face to face similar to those you use online? Or are they different? Explain.

Drama: How could you use oral and visual cues to help you interpret and understand a play? Which of the two types of cues do you think would be most useful? Why?

MY FIRST MILLION

Transcript from CBC News

Using Interpersonal Speaking Skills

Effective speakers realize that visual cues are important when communicating with an audience. What specific details tell the listener that Jacqueline Shan is aware of the importance of visual cues? Is her use of these cues appropriate for this oral text?

VOCABULARY

meningitis: an infection that causes the inflammation of the brain or spinal cord

prospective: expected; potential

Vocabulary Tip

Make connections to other words you know with the same prefix or suffix. For example, when you look at *meningitis* you might think of *appendicitis* or *arthritis*. This can help you figure out that the suffix has something to do with a disease.

This promotional video ran on the CBC network. It outlines Jacqueline Shan's journey from poor Chinese immigrant to successful scientist and entrepreneur. Jacqueline developed an innovative cold remedy and sold it with the help of well-known Canadian spokespeople.

COLD-FX is the #1 cold and flu brand in Canada.

JACQUELINE: I remember the first thing I told my prospective supervisor when I was a graduate student. He said, "Why do you think you can become a scientist?" I told him, "I think I am very imaginative." My name is Jacqueline Shan. I am the co-inventor of COLD-FX.

Her grandma treated her with herbal medicine.

JACQUELINE: When I was little, I used to get sick very often. One time I got meningitis. I was very curious about herbs, and dreamed that I would become a scientist so I could study herbs.

At age 23 she left China for Canada. She came to finish a Ph.D.

Using Oral and Visual Cues

To interpret oral text, analyze not only what the speaker is saying but also how he or she says it. What oral cues have been used by Jacqueline Shan in this text?

JACQUELINE: It was Boxing Day, I lost my coat, I barely spoke English, I had no money, and no one here to pick me up. So in the beginning, I was very panicked. So I looked around, finally I found an airport worker. So I used my broken English to get my message across, and so he showed me the public phone and gave me a quarter. I managed to make a call.

Don Cherry was a COLD-FX fan.

Using Interpersonal Speaking Skills

The type of interpersonal speaking strategies you use will influence the type of interactions you have with people. Who does Jacqueline perceive as her audience? Does she use a level of language that her audience can understand and respond to? Explain.

JACQUELINE: COLD-FX, from the beginning to the end, it cost us between 10 and 12 million dollars. In 2002 we almost went bankrupt. So I went to the board and said, "Please, I want to be the president, give me a chance. Let me try."

The company made $160 million in 4 years.

eBook Extra

Responding

What Do You Think Now? Is innovation the ability to see change as an opportunity instead of as a threat? How did Jacqueline Shan take advantage of change?

Understanding Listening and Speaking: Based on this script, what tone of voice do you believe is being used by Jacqueline Shan? Why do you think so?

Summarizing: If you had to write a one-sentence caption that would appear below Jacqueline Shan's photo on her website, what would you write?

Critical Thinking: What purpose does this video serve? Who is the intended audience?

Critical Literacy: How would a pharmacist, medical doctor, or naturopathic doctor respond to this text? Would their responses be the same or different? Explain.

Metacognition: While interacting with other people, what interpersonal listening and speaking strategies do you use? Do the types of strategies you use change to suit the person with whom you are interacting? Explain.

What Do You Think Now?

THINK BACK TO YOUR ORIGINAL RESPONSE TO THE STATEMENT: "HUMAN INNOVATION IMPROVES LIVES."

How have your feelings about this statement changed since you began this unit?

DEMONSTRATE YOUR LEARNING

Reflect on
* the texts you have read, viewed, and discussed during this unit
* the skills and strategies you have been developing

Select one of the following tasks to demonstrate your achievement of this unit's learning goals.

WRITE A BIOGRAPHY

Create a short biography (formal or contemporary) for someone you admire who had (or has) big ideas. Make sure you consider how your topic, purpose, and audience will influence your organization. Conduct research to make sure you know your topic thoroughly. Your biography should

☑ span the person's life
☑ provide details
☑ explain how the person's ideas affected others
☑ include quotations
☑ address whether the person was innovative

PANEL DISCUSSION OF BIG IDEAS

With a small group, discuss this unit and the big ideas you've read about. Together, research and decide which idea was the biggest and what makes an idea big. Remember to

☑ use oral and visual cues as you speak and as you listen to others speak
☑ speak at a controlled pace
☑ involve others in the discussion
☑ stay on topic

PRODUCE A VIDEO NEWSCAST

On your own or with a group, create a five-minute newscast on the theme of this unit—big ideas. To create the newscast, develop scripts for three or four stories that will interest your audience. Be sure to

☑ develop and organize your main ideas
☑ use oral and visual cues appropriate for a newscast
☑ use the conventions and techniques commonly found in a TV newscast

Selections Grouped by Theme and Form

Index

Credits